Beyond Survival of the Fattest

The economics of smart little helpers over stupid great shysters

By Jose T Manic

For comment and discussion:
www.utternomics.com

Acknowledgements

The author is totally indebted to Alex and Richard for their criticism and encouragement and to all those, like Nick, who ask "Are you sure there isn't more to it than they say?"

Contents

Jose Manic

Introduction

In the 1980's, as we witnessed the fall of the Berlin wall, we were excited by the prospect and speed of change. And not through a mob but by a rapidly rising tide. The old world order was being dismantled by hand, by citizens. At the same time in the west we saw the dismantling of state controlled industries and the marketing of a new political ideology that would become neoliberalism. My own optimism for the prospect of state controlled socialism at that time gave out to an interest in private enterprise and the science of evolution. The argument against centralised planning and for free competition had apparently been won.

Now, in 2014, anyone arguing that our system is adequate for the task of providing goods and services and sufficient honest work and justice, probably has a vested interest. And yet the main criticism levelled at those seeking change today is that there are no alternative economic systems. This is not true, but as Michael Moore puts it, capitalism is an 18th century idea and communism a 19th century idea – we could use some new ideas!

I have given the alternative put forward in this book an ism too. This is not out of a desire to launch a Portunist movement or to define an ideology, but so that serious debate on alternative systems can no longer be avoided by those naysayers. That debate is long overdue. We cannot afford to wait much longer. This is why the fictional story in this book is short, and the non-fiction parts are intended to be digestible and non-technical. You can read only the fiction or non-fiction parts if you prefer. The message is just as pressing and either one is about as long as a Michael Moore film.

This book provides a view of what could be possible. We need a little fiction to give us a new perspective on what sort of morass we are in and to help imagine how we might crawl out of it. The fiction parts (Part 1 and Part 3) in their portrayal of an optimistic future beyond neoliberalism, could become fact. While the factual, non-fiction parts (Part 2 and Part 4) travel through alternative worlds to show how we evolved to be mired in a stagnating economic system of amassing fat and waste. The good news is that the same light that reveals the evolutionary cause of our problems could finally illuminate an exit.

Beyond Survival of the Fattest

Part 1. Interviewing Dystopia

One

The wind across the roof of the sixty story News Media International building pulled at the Editor's breath. He was not standing on the roof, but on the metal and brick wall around the edge of the roof, feet hooked under the railing on top of that, cold hands clasping the dusty steel rail that was pressed against the top of his thighs making orange marks on his suit. His eyes watered in the wind that was vibrating the back of his suit jacket and his head was buzzing.

Top heavy as he was, a life-long frequenter of gyms, restaurants and taxis, this was a real physical risk. Not the office-bound, word-playing, money-making, power-gaming, that never quite seems to satisfy risk, but the one false move or freak gust and you're dead kind of risk. The kind to play with. He looked down and, with the kick of cognisance, a wave flowed through the nerves in his feet, up out of a pit down below and into his head so fast that he almost lost it.

"Jesus!" He snapped out and turned round to a new sound. Climbing down just in time as his younger colleague opened the stair well door, he took control of the conversation before it started.

"This city has been here 2000 years. You know that Frank?"

The younger colleague started to doubt the timing of his approach but quickly recalibrated and smiled as he walked towards his boss. Obviously he was in one of his moods.

"And what the hell is it coming to?" asked the Editor.

"When the whole world is an asylum it's the psychopaths who will succeed?" offered the colleague.

"Never in my life have I seen so much newsworthy strife and mess. This is an interesting time for us. It's not like there isn't good stuff for you to write about. People want answers Frank. Give them the real story, not some hoax message from the future!"

The Editor started to make for the mouth of the stair well.

"And I'm not going to read it. You have until we get to my office. I've been interviewing those little interns all afternoon and, frankly, their damned enthusiasm and idealism..." He spat the words out. "..has worn me down and given me a bloody awful headache. Anyway, I do not see how we can make this remotely credible. Messages from the future?"

The Editor rolled his eyes as the younger man held open the jaw to the stairs.

So the younger man explained and the older man

listened for a while as they dropped into the warm honeycomb of the building. But when he had explained, the Editor was not excited like the younger man. He was unhappy. What a lovely idea. How hopeless must a person be in this age that they would hang on to such a pathetic dream of equality and justice. How depressingly desperate and pitiful.

Nevertheless, he took home the message to read. There, it was his turn to explain.

*

"No, I am going to stay up a bit, love. I thought I would read this article. It's from the future."

"That'll be fun for you then. Don't wake me when you come up."

Chapter 7 of 'Writing for New Order Magazine' was 'The Secrets of Dr J Littlebelle'. It was the Editor's normal habit to dip in about a third way into a piece to check the tone and interest level and he found this.

"How bad could free enterprise have been, if people were still economically free in the "free-market" sense? Big business being constantly kept honest by a never ending stream of challenges from new small businesses and the attending new opportunities for workers? Is that what you mean?"

"The point is that you contradict yourself by advocating enterprise and competition while claiming to oppose the old free-market capitalism."

"Okay. Some people do point to the little companies that did exist. Yes, that should have provided some source of hope and novel solutions. But if those tiny saplings could break through the thick canopy created by the industrial giants they could only do it by taking full advantage of the permissiveness of neoliberalism. Yes, there were opportunities for the new to break through, but only if they were to harvest the huge rewards available to those who exploit, manipulate and abuse, those who tap into human-kind's most primitive instincts and weaknesses.

"How bad could businesses get? Only the usurers, pornographers, bookmakers and pimps could succeed because in a habitat where anything is for sale, where, in order to protect the interests of the vast pyramids, a philosophy is spun that permits no obstacle to selling anything, any person or moral value, it is the exploitation, prostitution and enslaving of people that is the most profitable. Business was an evil word. Profit was not the natural surplus from valuable human endeavour, the measure of success in delivering value to the world and a store for future investment for mankind's benefit, as it is today, but in people's minds only synonymous with profiteering and extortion. That is just what business had become."

The editor did not know or care who Dr J

Littlebelle was and already cared for his politics even less. But, as this was a view from the future, perhaps the doctor's time did justify such an extremist rant. He decided to give it a chance and turned to the start of the chapter, almost regretting it straightaway.

*

> On this pungent and oppressive July evening, I was not really looking forward to this assignment..

"Jesus wept! I hope she isn't writing for me in the future" said the Editor out loud.

But as he ploughed through the flowery text he began to warm to the young writer. The writing was average, but she had a good attitude for a journalist he thought. He liked them young and feisty and he imagined she was attractive, as they usually were at that age. At least the ones who he hired were. She described parts of her early career and the Editor related to the frustration of trying to make an impression and a difference in the face of rejection and apathy. For him, it was a distant memory he had almost blocked out, but for her it seemed, it was a personal test that she delighted in.

She had the job of interviewing ancient relics - academics and activists in economics. The Editor could not imagine anything more dull. Her pieces and the angle had not been her choice. Some dramatic change had taken place in their recent past and it was assumed she would write about it supportively. The Editor thought her counter argument had won out with: "Surely interviews are for questioning things?"

The Editor liked the girl. But it was harder to make out the interviewee. She was also sceptical about him. The other revolutionary interviewees had been clear-cut, earnest hardliners with a simple message. But this one had a reputation for equivocation and compromise. Now, well into the twilight of a career that had once been glorious and fanatical, she wondered if she should be trying to lift the lid on him or the movement that had promoted his ideas, or even if there was anything left to reveal. In the end she decided to focus on a principle question: Had they gone too far or not far enough?

Two

Travelling to the assignment, she described the end of an elongated summer and a journey from the city to the country as if it were a trip back in time itself. This cosy old chap lived alone in a snug rural house which had a view out the back where combines were whisking up gold dust in the early evening sun.

We continued talking on a bright terrace at the back of his house and, as we shared the wine I had brought, as I often did on interviews, we began to settle a little in the evening sunshine. I leant forward to move the microphone a little closer, wanting to catch everything and this is where the transcript starts:

"...It's my pleasure now, of course. But back then I received far too much personal attention. There seemed to be an interview every day. Now it's all nearly forgotten. But back then in that age..."

"The age of the pyramids you called it?" I had read quite a bit for this interview.

"That's right." He smiled, looking pleased with

me. To start with I just encouraged him to talk.

"In those days everything was organised in pyramids" he continued. "People wanted to get to the top of the heap and if they succeeded they used their influence to gain wealth and power."

"You mean influence and wealth just for themselves?" I asked.

"Is that so hard to imagine? You write historical pieces don't you?" I think he was wondering how hard the explaining was going to be.

I understood perfectly well but I did learn a lot from the assignment. I had heard the historical perspective before. Why, back then, a man or woman would try to accumulate huge wealth, how status and hierarchy dominated the culture, what it must have felt like in those brutish times, trying to scale invisible pyramids and then suddenly the pyramids, the futility and the waste being revealed.

We had a decent look at the history, but I also managed to get some insights into the movement that changed it and the personalities involved. And later, it even looked like I had stumbled on an unexpected revelation.

As I interviewed him, he explained what it was like in the manner of a teacher. Which is part of what he was of course. He walked me through those tides of change. On occasions his wistfulness was infectious and palpable.

"Jesus!" said the editor, out loud again, but settling

down in the darkening room.

"Why don't you just set the scene for me?" I asked. "Is it possible to sum up why things had gone so wrong and why the change had to come then?"

"Like I said, everything was pyramids. We get pyramids automatically. It's human nature. It is even *in* nature. Complexity can organise if there are ascending layers like a pyramid. Lots of things, not just human organisations. Complex machines do it with hierarchies of components, genetics does it, even words on a page, with letters being arranged into syllables, syllables into words, words into phrases, phrases into sentences. Do you see? It is a good way for complexity to be broken down. People organise themselves into such hierarchies, even today. It is just that now our business pyramids are smaller and the forces driving unbounded expansion of the pyramids are no longer there. They don't need to be. Genetics is not a power structure, neither are words on a page. They just need each other."

"Carry on."

"One of the root causes of the problems at that time was due to the way people give authority to those above them. That authority instinct is natural but it can lead to a false sense of ownership. Those pyramids were huge not for the good of the organisation. Businesses can take advantage of a pyramidal structure, but this was different. The pyramids had evolved, and I mean literally evolved, into huge lumbering dinosaurs. The evolutionary process had gone badly wrong."

"I would like to come back to the role of evolution in all this, if we can. Because that was the key to the cure as well as the cause, wasn't it? But one of your points was that some non-living things, as you say, "literally evolve", right?"

"Yes, of course. The knowledge to make non-living populations evolve has been around since John Holland in the 1970's."

"Okay. But can you set the scene for before the Change? You know our readership is quite young and it is the old attitudes that are very often hard for people to understand. We see ourselves as being more enlightened now, but people were not stupid back then. I mean, with respect, it's hard to see how people back then could get it so hopelessly wrong. Can we explore why, what seems like basic backwardness now, used to seem like the only possible way?"

"Well first of all, yes, I hope we are more enlightened. But cultures can change dramatically simply because their perspective, their point of view, is just that – looking at the world from one point. This is always limited. We are never as enlightened or as objective as we feel we are. Yes, people have not become smarter as individuals in a few generations, but the perspectives which they take on the world have changed hugely. It is as the sociologist Pierre Bordieu explained, given a particular   perspective   Social   Silences   are everywhere. So much is hidden from us. The Social Silences, the things that we do not read about, or talk of, or consider, are what really control us. And we are long sighted. The closer something is to us, the less likely we are to see it.

"And tragically, objectivity will rarely come from experts either. It is especially absent in the media and the printed word. They are a product of the same society. And worse, they will inevitably fight any change in the language and terms used to define the social space. As a journalist you perpetuate this because these terms and symbols are your stock-in-trade and since they are passed down to you, you are bound to conform. Getting either silence or the response 'That's not how we talk about that' can make enlightenment very difficult."

"Well ok. But do you think you can help me piece together what that old perspective was then?"

"I may be some use there" he smiled. "As I lived through it, it never seemed alien to me. Just..." He paused. "...broken". He briefly looked sad, perhaps at all the lost years, I don't know, then smiled into my eyes again. I thought I should narrow the question.

"Okay. So about the pyramids. For them to evolve that way, I believe there had to be a confusion   and   interchangeability   between businesses and people, right? How could that culture confuse the two? How can a society that believes itself to be civilised treat a human being the same way as a canning machine or a forklift robot?"

This was not a naïve question. I knew that the folks-firms confusion was the crux of the problem in the old days. I just did not understand how such a mistake could go unnoticed for two centuries.

"Well, first of all you must understand that such convolutions are very common in human organisation through history. Mankind has learned, adapted and applied many kinds of Portunism in the past, way before Economic Portunism – the splitting of the two economies. But just take one example: the church and the state. They used to be inextricably linked in Europe. Should it have been obvious to medieval England, say, that they should be separated?"

"You might think so" I said. "One is about a personal faith and philosophy of life and the other is about deciding and implementing rules for a nation. I never quite understood that confusion either."

"No, it could not be obvious. Because both of those realms are about leading people. Leaders came about, so they led. Sometimes religiously, sometimes militarily, sometimes economically. But also religion was so important and religious practice and conformism so near and dear to people, that would have left a huge Social Silence. No one would dare talk about ruling without religion. The society only made the distinction when the problems those two realms caused each other became unbearable."

"But canning machines and employees?"

"It's exactly the same. They are both means of production. People and machinery or automation had never been deliberately separated in businesses, so it never occurred to anyone that there were two distinct systems at work. But you do realise that the intertwining at that level was not the main problem?"

"Please expand, if you would like to."

"Okay. Having the same economic status as canning machines, as strange and wicked as it may seem to you, was only an unfortunate side effect. The damaging intertwining between the two realms of firms and folks was higher up the pyramid. This is where those in authority were also rewarded in proportion to that authority. The guy, and it was nearly always a man back then, at the top of the pyramid, partly because of his influence and partly because of history, was, in people's minds, entitled to a slice of the action of the whole pyramid. That is if you were at the top. If you were half way you were entitled to a slice of those layers below you, and so on."

"But why, when people are basically working for the same thing in an enterprise?"

"Because the reward pressures on people had evolved a certain culture, and certain type of person."

"Well this is what I am trying to understand.

What was the culture that would support that?"

"Okay. You said you wanted to come back to evolution, so I won't dwell on this, but you must understand this much. Two populations right? Evolution only needs three things, competition, copying and a diverse population. For one of the populations – the evolving population of enterprises – you can probably imagine the evolution that is going on. They compete with each other, they retain and reproduce successes, failures die off, there is diversity. Excellent! But the unnoticed evolving population is that of the employee/worker. There is also diversity, retention of successful practices, failure dying off, certainly competition for jobs. But what is the reward mechanism here?"

"Terms and conditions, job satisfaction and recognition?"

He smiled at this for some reason.

"Sure. It was a little narrower in those days. Mostly just about pay I am afraid, but yes. But how do you think the firm will see the financial rewarding if the structure is a giant pyramid and the higher up you go in it the greater is the chance for success or failure of the firm? If an employee's influence is large, the cost of having the wrong person in that position could be high. So businesses competed for the best person – as they do today of course - but without any restrictions, the price paid will rise and rise. Especially as the supply of human resources is so inelastic. In other words it takes decades to train a person and for them to acquire the right experience. The supply cannot quickly increase to meet demand. So for high influence positions, in the absence of restrictions, the price can shoot up practically without limit."

"But that is so unequal. I do not understand why people would tolerate it?"

He paused and then, instead of answering, more or less pounced on the notebook I was holding, grabbing my hand and pen in the process.

"Do you mind? Can I show you one thing?"

Holding the notebook to the table in front of me he drew these two figures.

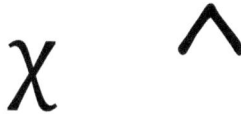

$$\chi \qquad \wedge$$

"I used to teach it like this. The stick man is a human worker with all his potential for adding value. This one has 4 connection points through which he can connect with other employees in his enterprise - five if you add his head. This one.." pointing the pen at the chevron "is the specialised species we had evolved into. He is more limited. You can imagine him as just two strong arms manipulating and grabbing at everything beneath him. A reward system with no upward limit as you ascend the pyramid will evolve this type of creature. And, as Ha-Joon Chang had shown, economics drives culture, not the other way round. So these highly adapted creatures did not care too much about equality. Partly they were accustomed to inequality, but also, frankly, most of the time they - 'we' I should probably say - were all far too focussed on our own little pyramid to notice."

My mind was protesting at this concept and I was about to protest his rudeness too, as he sat back with my notebook in hand.

"May I have a page?" He said, while tearing from the back of my pad. For the next few minutes he was drawing on the paper and looking up at me only occasionally. An opportunity to make the obvious counter argument.

"But it is not just unequal, it is also unjust. If you are working in a less influential position you may have been through years of training too. In a good business everyone is working for the same end. I have heard stories about the inequality of the time, and I know there must be some exaggeration, but I do not understand how people – the non-privileged ones – would tolerate it?" This was one of the areas where I could not help wondering if self-interest had coloured his own politics.

"That is a very good question. And what you have heard is probably no exaggeration. The rich and powerful genuinely could earn a thousand times more than someone actually delivering the services in the same company. And those at the bottom did genuinely suffer as a result; poorer health, poor housing or no home at all, a slavish work-life if they could get work, minimal freedoms, prejudice and inadequate education, shorter life span. The list goes on. And they would work right alongside people with enough to keep them in luxury for a hundred lifetimes. But the intolerable was more tolerated then." he said a little mysteriously, still looking down and drawing.

He stopped and sighed, before continuing with the most outrageous explanation I have heard.

"There is one simple reason that is probably not so obvious to your generation. The people who said that the lucky ones were not just lucky, that they actually earned their rewards, that they were hard working and superior in many ways, the people who claimed that, were, in some ways, right."

He paused to see how shocked I was to hear him say that. I tried not to show it.

"Such an evolving system is self-fulfilling you see. Those higher positions, through the process of competition will, by and large, be given to the most talented and capable people. That is a fact of competition in the labour market, the same as today. It does not seem so unjust if the guy above you actually is smarter and more hardworking. You could argue that it was hard to be a top chevron.

"So, for example, our society needed elite education for some and very basic education for others. Therefore, in a vicious circle, it also needed businesses which required a significant amount of organising and managing so those elite could be brought in along with their talents. Whole industries and professions would evolve that were focussed on the abstraction, analysis and sophistications for exerting influence over large numbers of others. That kind of work was much more prized than directly delivering the services the business was there for. The whole means of production evolved to become over technological, over complex and on a larger scale simply in order to get the best people in the company. That was the type of employment firms had to offer to get the more skilled and able."

"So that was all hunky dory? People were happy with those levels of inequality?"

"Well, no, not to the degree we had it obviously. But it made a significant degree of inequality seem almost fair."

I had a problem with this. Not only because I thought he was wrong, but because it made him one of them rather than one of us. His level of sympathy with the old capitalist system was suspicious I thought. He saw my distaste and tried again.

"The other side to it, is that if you are the business paying the excessive rewards you naturally want a lot back. The elite from my time were not the same as the elite from before the world wars, for example, where their entitlements had more or less fallen in their lap. Most of those at the top in my day *did* have to work for their excessive wealth, and often work hard. This all meant that it was possible to make the argument that was around at the time. Which was 'Okay, I have a lot more than you – but, hey, I am actually smarter than you and I have worked damned hard to get where I am'."

"Isn't that a bit outrageous? People would see what was going on surely?"

"Well, it is in the nature of those aspiring - and aspirations in those days were mostly about wealth and influence, as I have said - in the nature of those aspiring to look up, admire and copy those above them, and not to challenge those superior to their position. Likewise, it is in the interest of the influential to convince as many people as possible that they *should* be aspiring, to want to be like those at the top and that they *can* climb a few rungs up the ladder. So, yes, many people did see it as almost fair. Or at least sufficiently fair to have a go at climbing rather than taking to the streets."

We looked at each other as he took a drink of wine. It was obviously a little uncomfortable for him to have to admit his generation's sins. But I was coming to the conclusion that he had been one of those elite himself for much of his life. It was at this point that I started to sense other forces at work and thought I should look more into the man and his story.

He pushed the piece of paper with his sketches on towards me.

Jose Manic

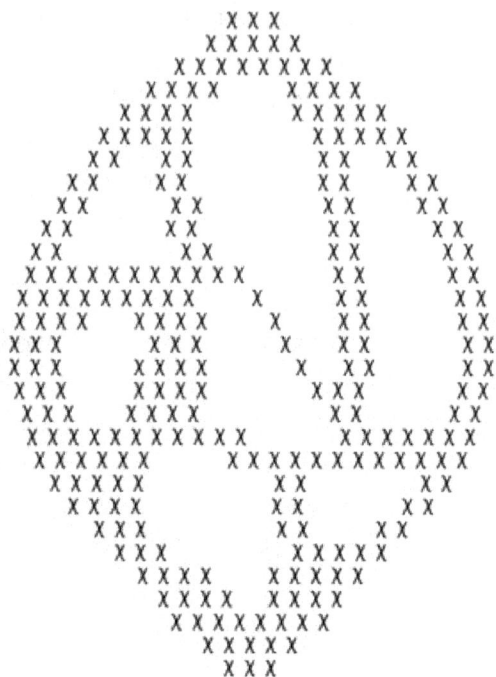

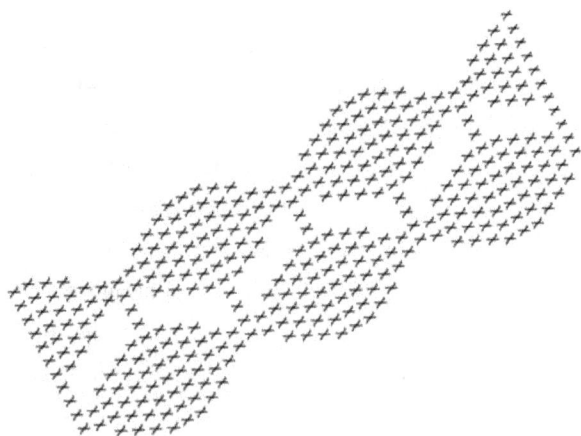

Beyond Survival of the Fattest

"There. You see these two structures? These
are from recent analyses of company structures of
today. We see that one..." [pointing to the first
sketch - these taken from a later publication] "...in
close clusters of companies. This one [the second
sketch] is common in manufacturing and supply
chain industries. But there are lots of successful
structures now evolving. Clever little critters that are
agile, multifaceted and expert at networking with
other companies. We do not know exactly why these
particular geometries work, but they do, and with a
variety and rate of change that is extraordinary. But
these structures are only possible with a largely non-
hierarchical approach. You see they are made up
from the highly networked stick people?

He continued in whimsical teacher mode as I
looked.

"Now what type of structures do you think you
can make with the highly specialised Mr and Ms
Chevron?" As he said this, he turned the page over:

```
                                        ^
                                      ^ ^ ^
                                    ^ ^ ^ ^ ^
                                  ^ ^ ^ ^ ^ ^ ^
                                ^ ^ ^ ^ ^ ^ ^ ^ ^
                              ^ ^ ^ ^ ^ ^ ^ ^ ^ ^ ^
                            ^ ^ ^ ^ ^ ^ ^ ^ ^ ^ ^ ^ ^
                          ^ ^ ^ ^ ^ ^ ^ ^ ^ ^ ^ ^ ^ ^ ^
                        ^ ^ ^ ^ ^ ^ ^ ^ ^ ^ ^ ^ ^ ^ ^ ^ ^
                      ^ ^ ^ ^ ^ ^ ^ ^ ^ ^ ^ ^ ^ ^ ^ ^ ^ ^ ^
                    ^ ^ ^ ^ ^ ^ ^ ^ ^ ^ ^ ^ ^ ^ ^ ^ ^ ^ ^ ^ ^
                  ^ ^ ^ ^ ^ ^ ^ ^ ^ ^ ^ ^ ^ ^ ^ ^ ^ ^ ^ ^ ^ ^ ^
                ^ ^ ^ ^ ^ ^ ^ ^ ^ ^ ^ ^ ^ ^ ^ ^ ^ ^ ^ ^ ^ ^ ^ ^ ^
              ^ ^ ^ ^ ^ ^ ^ ^ ^ ^ ^ ^ ^ ^ ^ ^ ^ ^ ^ ^ ^ ^ ^ ^ ^ ^ ^
            ^ ^ ^ ^ ^ ^ ^ ^ ^ ^ ^ ^ ^ ^ ^ ^ ^ ^ ^ ^ ^ ^ ^ ^ ^ ^ ^ ^ ^
          ^ ^ ^ ^ ^ ^ ^ ^ ^ ^ ^ ^ ^ ^ ^ ^ ^ ^ ^ ^ ^ ^ ^ ^ ^ ^ ^ ^ ^ ^ ^
        ^ ^ ^ ^ ^ ^ ^ ^ ^ ^ ^ ^ ^ ^ ^ ^ ^ ^ ^ ^ ^ ^ ^ ^ ^ ^ ^ ^ ^ ^ ^ ^ ^
      ^ ^ ^ ^ ^ ^ ^ ^ ^ ^ ^ ^ ^ ^ ^ ^ ^ ^ ^ ^ ^ ^ ^ ^ ^ ^ ^ ^ ^ ^ ^ ^ ^ ^ ^
    ^ ^ ^ ^ ^ ^ ^ ^ ^ ^ ^ ^ ^ ^ ^ ^ ^ ^ ^ ^ ^ ^ ^ ^ ^ ^ ^ ^ ^ ^ ^ ^ ^ ^ ^ ^ ^
  ^ ^ ^ ^ ^ ^ ^ ^ ^ ^ ^ ^ ^ ^ ^ ^ ^ ^ ^ ^ ^ ^ ^ ^ ^ ^ ^ ^ ^ ^ ^ ^ ^ ^ ^ ^ ^ ^ ^
^ ^ ^ ^ ^ ^ ^ ^ ^ ^ ^ ^ ^ ^ ^ ^ ^ ^ ^ ^ ^ ^ ^ ^ ^ ^ ^ ^ ^ ^ ^ ^ ^ ^ ^ ^ ^ ^ ^ ^ ^
```

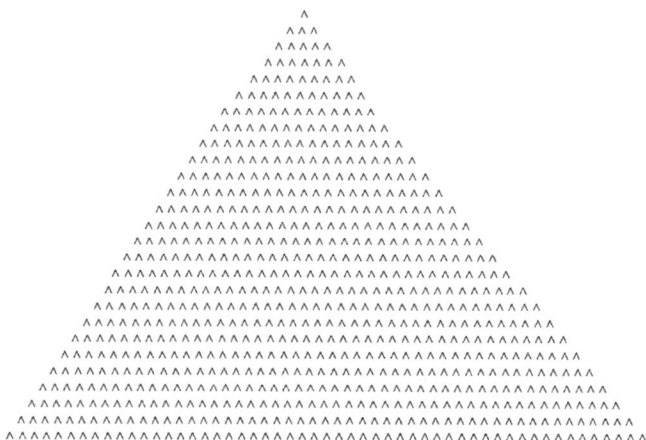

"I will tell you. This structure. Or, over time, a bigger pyramid. Or, if you wait longer still, much bigger, and so on until they are pretty much pushing at the limits of planet Earth."

Three

The Editor took a large sip of whiskey as he read on with the young journalist continuing.

"If that describes the culture and the mentality of people before the Change, you are basically saying they accepted a lot of crap because they did not know any better and because it did have at least a degree of fairness."

"That isn't a bad way of putting it."

This made me both angry and suspicious.

"But what was your story, I wonder? Before we get onto the conclusions that you came to, can you tell me how your life came to converge with the radical change that was about to happen? In fact, perhaps we can start before that. How did your career start?"

"My life is not very interesting and not something up for discussion – as I said on the phone."

I held my tongue waiting for more.

"But, as you wish. I had a fairly rural childhood.

Mother was the first in the family to be educated, we followed. When I went to Cambridge I had gained a great interest in the natural world. In any case, after travelling widely and working in Bonn for the son of a shoe maker, my ideas and research took me into biology and then evolution and then, naturally perhaps, to evolutionary economics. That's it."

"So you didn't go straight into research after university or after your early career. Not a pure academic?"

"No."

Another long pause.

"After those travels, when I returned I had another career in mind initially. But it is not interesting."

"Oh really. What?"

"Well, I actually thought I would become a journalist and worked at that for a while."

"How fascinating!" I was genuinely pleased, partly because this was not in the biographies but also, to my discredit, I started to think I could trust him after all, on account of the common ground between us. "I don't think that's documented anywhere."

"That is because nothing happened" another pause as he inexplicably winced and rubbed the top of his arm, as if he had just been injected or was recalling a painful sting. "Actually I did say on the phone we would not cover my personal life. If you don't mind. It really is irrelevant."

Beyond Survival of the Fattest

I had enough journalist's intuition to think otherwise.

"Were you a good enough journalist? Is that why you went back to academia?" I asked.

"Not particularly." he grinned. "That has a lot to do with it. Very incisive of you."

He was not getting away with it that easily.

"But you went on to make a career out of writing and exploring ideas and arguments, very successfully. I wonder what you have against my profession that made you turn against it?"

"It really wasn't like that. I just moved on."

"Or ran away?"

I was amazed when he stood up.

"I have told you I do not wish to discuss it. And this sort of prying is precisely what people have against your profession, as you call it. Not only the persistent rudeness, but the consistent failure to see what is really important. You people." he shook his head. "Do you know that society's view with all its gaps and Social Silences disseminates from, and is perpetuated largely by the industry of the printed word? I did come to despise it, because of what it holds back. Yes, I tried and failed as a journalist. That was not a problem to me. It simply dawned on me that the masters in that industry would never see the new and would never let go of the old. My offers to provide some new objective commentary were usually met with one of those famous silences. But thank goodness I persisted. One night I woke up and saw clearly for the first time that commentary and words piled on words were not enough...."

He was glaring at me. I was anxious to clear the atmosphere in case he terminated the interview.

"It is a brutal industry. They would not have appreciated you back then." I paused while he sat down again. "I just wondered if it was something specific in your philosophy that made you return to the subject of evolutionary economics?" I asked.

"No, nothing like that. As a matter of fact the inspiration for Portunism – the need I felt to find the way to separate the evolution of firms from the evolution of people - you could say was inspired by journalism."

He looked up, considered and stood up again.

"I think that will be all for today."

That was a pity, but I was not going to forget that little nugget.

Four

What stuck with me while returning to the city was not so much Dr Littlebelle's history, although I had some intuition it was relevant, but his surprising level of tolerance for the injustices of the old ways. At that time there were many that were saying that the Change had not gone far enough, that any capitalism was noxious and dangerous and would eventually grow to dominate and oppress us again. I could not help wondering if Littlebelle had helped preserve aspects of the old system in order to preserve himself. When I reviewed my research I was even more suspicious.

The starting point for interviews was always old news clippings as well as biographies and recorded accounts. But armed with some knowledge of the person, I took another look at the old news items and this time noticed two patterns.

Firstly, there was something different in the press vilification he had received. Collectively, all prominent challengers of the old economic order were anarchists, layabouts, communists, new-age hippies, hypocrites and the like. I began to categorise and chart them according to the type of criticism. "Hypocrite" came up a lot more for Littlebelle and there was something quite different about the criticism he received.

Whereas most of the economic activators were accused of being dangerous because of their extremism and commercial naivety, he was nearly always attacked for being somehow fake. Unverified accusations about deceptions in his personal life, stories about the movement not trusting him with funds, about him harbouring a secret love of capitalism. Even the photographs had a pattern to them. He was nearly always caught at the moment where he was looking shifty-eyed or with those around him sharing knowing glances. It looked exactly like a contrivance by enemies, but why that angle? And then I noticed from a few papers the names cropping up: "The faker" and "The phoney". Where did they get that idea?

Secondly, when I put it all in chronological order, all that propaganda, the accusations of hypocrisy and the insinuations, they all came to a point in time then just stopped. How did that happen?

Part of my recent training was about not biasing your own investigations with premature theories. But on the journey back to the lonely cottage in the country for the second interview, I could not help speculating on what forces had been against him and what forces were at his command.

The Editor poured another whiskey.

At the start of the second interview we soon resumed close to where we had left off. Judging his mood, I decided that if I eased into the angle I was really after he would have seen through it and could have an excuse to terminate. I did not want another terminator. I wanted to know what had happened with him but also to explore what affection he really held for the old system.

"Perhaps we can restart with what happened in the development of your work, back at university, when your ideas started to interest radical political groups. Without prying into anything personal, I would like to understand a little of your own motivation. I mean, you have explained how society was mostly accepting of the old order, but not you. Due to some inspiration or other, you focussed your research on alternative systems. Why the dire need, given what you have said? I mean, okay, you had long concluded that the evolution of two clashing systems was the root problem, but, you know, the system was still functioning wasn't it? I mean how bad could it be? You dedicated your life to developing an alternative to the old capitalism. Why was that even necessary?"

"How bad could it be?"

I nodded and waited while he mustered up the

patience he seemed to need.

"Well okay then. It's like this. We were talking about how enterprises were evolving to become larger and larger. In fact, in the latter years, that happened very quickly and the results were truly shocking. In the case of enterprise size, it is a very direct Lamarkian adaptation. Which I can also explain if you wish?"

I ignored the loaded 'also'.

"Please."

"So, even before evolutionary economics was recognised, it was a well understood conundrum in economics that shareholders want profit but managers want growth. If you are a manager and your rewards are directly proportional to your influence, living on a pyramid, everything starts to be about attaining growth. As I said, with that type of reward pressure, over the generations, even the institutions such as in education will adapt to the bloated system. But with growth, the decisions of managers act quickly. The decision to have the merger, to go for market share rather than niche, to find economies in scale rather than adaptable production. They all happen so quickly that a globalized oligopoly takes over so fast that it sends people into shock."

"But surely the diseconomies of scale would stop businesses from growing too much, too quickly. I mean those pyramids are simply less efficient the bigger they get. We learnt basic allometry at primary school."

"Well, yes. It actually depends on the networks within the pyramid, and that was understood by many. Nevertheless diseconomies of scale were rarely mentioned. Business people and economists more often talked about the '*economies* of scale'…"

He paused before continuing. I guessed he had used the same phrase in the past to shock his students into paying attention.

"…'Economy of scale' is an affect that is seen sometimes in production. Many commodities and high volume manufacturing benefit from it. It was an important phenomenon during and after the 2nd world war. You know, to build the tanks and pump the oil on the greatest possible scale. But in my day the principle was applied to everything. Despite incontrovertible evidence from people like Geoffrey West that the diseconomies of growth far out-weigh the advantages."

"So big businesses were thought to be *more* productive?"

"Exactly. And again it is not so hard to understand why. Again there is a self-fulfilling affect. An example would be consumer packaged goods. The two dominating companies…"

Again a short pause and look, so he could enjoy my incredulity.

"….could outcompete by wasting huge resources and brain power with expensive but highly competitive products. They would literally hire the best and greatest number of scientific minds in the country and put them on crucial tasks such as designing a new deodorant top, or computer modelling a flushing toilet. The fact is that people will buy more deodorant with the latest advanced locking cap, despite it adding no value to society or the consumer, and the success of their products against smaller rivals was conveniently described as an 'economy of scale'. Of course it was nothing of the sort. It was a near-monopoly exercising power over the labour force to preserve its market domination."

We shared a pained smile and now he wanted to continue.

"But the point is that growth of the pyramids had been very fast. In 1855 there were 500 clearing banks in Great Britain and by 1955 just 5. But the pace really picked up after that. By the end of that century diversity and competition was already dying out. Typically there would have been four to seven companies dominating in almost every major industry. As the century went on, so did the agglomeration and pretty soon all was stagnation, corporate oppression and cultural and economic poverty. You ask how bad could it get? Let me describe some of it. Better still, try to imagine how it must have been."

I did not try to stop or deflect him.

"How can a system that uses evolution to solve problems - to add value, to ensure continued support for its hard working citizens – how can it have that evolutionary system grow into such a tumorous, deformed monster that it fails in all of those things? How can that be anything but bad?

"As those huge pyramids grew ocean spanning legs and sprawled continents they stifled every piece of creativity, innovation and humanity. Evolution needs diversity, competition and inheritance. That's all. Never mind that, human beings need diversity as much as they need competition. With a few behemoths dominating, for example, food supply, medicine, energy and finance, diversity and quality of life was gone.

"Take their beloved car industry..." he looked ridiculous as he paused to laugh. "...to think we couldn't understand why the innovations had dried up. No practical solutions to the mounting and deadly pollution had come out for decades. But it was no wonder. Those dinosaurs no longer even knew how to design a new car. They had lost the ability. As they teetered on the edge of extinction the only commercial advantage they had was the money they could borrow due to the fear they instilled from the prospect of their bankrupt demise and the economic decay that would spread from it. With that extorted finance they could make a meagre profit by lending more to the world's over-consumers. Forget even trying to make a profit from making cars! That had long gone. But they limped on and continued their stranglehold on progress, stifling all alternative means of transport while simultaneously, like a never-ending chemical weapons attack, destroying the health of entire nations.

"How bad could it get you say? Were people healthy and living well? Was there anything physically healthy for them left in their environment? Following almost the whole of the history of mankind with food and health improving, we had started to slide, then tumble, then plummet backwards. With all production and food processing in the hands of a few pyramids, food was at one end of the supply chain a commodity to be traded for profit and to oppress farmers around the world, and at the other, a manufactured product to be churned out at the lowest possible cost, at best nutrition free, and more often accumulatively poisonous.

"And how bad can our use of energy and natural resource get? Natural resources up in smoke with the people becoming sick on the fumes and waste. There was none of the innovation we have today in alternative supplies, safe post-nuclear power generation, Web Photovoltaic Cell production or local fermentation. With no diversity and creativity to speak of, and competition stifled by a handful of omniscient energy companies, all we knew was how to pump more from the ground until the earth heaved and withered.

I had to barge in. I was dying to know who or what did he blame for these failings.

Beyond Survival of the Fattest

"Okay, we all know that there were problems to fix, but you argued that the capitalist system that caused the problems could also be used to solve them. How could you argue for a hugely disruptive change in the fundamentals of the old free-market system and then advocate replacing it with a new form of free enterprise? We have free enterprise now that seems to work well. So why did you claim you were so against it back then?

"How bad could free enterprise have been, if people were still economically free in the "free-market" sense? Big business being constantly kept honest by a never ending stream of challenges from new small businesses and the attending new opportunities for workers? Is that what you mean?"

"The point is that you contradict yourself by advocating enterprise and competition while claiming to oppose the old free-market capitalism."

"Okay. Some people do point to the little companies that did exist. Yes, that should have provided some source of hope and novel solutions. But if those tiny saplings could break through the thick canopy created by the industrial giants they could only do it by taking full advantage of the permissiveness of neoliberalism. Yes, there were opportunities for the new to break through, but only if they were to harvest the huge rewards available to those who exploit, manipulate and abuse, those who tap into human-kind's most primitive instincts and weaknesses.

"How bad could businesses get? Only the usurers, pornographers, bookmakers and pimps could succeed because in a habitat where anything is for sale, where, in order to protect the interests of the vast pyramids a philosophy is spun that permits no obstacle to selling anything, any person or moral value, it is the exploitation, prostitution and enslaving of people that is the most profitable. Business was an evil word. Profit was not the natural surplus from valuable human endeavour, the measure of success in delivering value to the world and a store for future investment for mankind's benefit, as it is today, but in people's minds only synonymous with profiteering and extortion. That is just what business had become. But more terrible than that, if you can imagine it, with diversity gone leaving a trail of exploitation, sickness with nothing affordable or of quality for people to eat, and that barren overcrowded and polluted moonscape for a habitat, there was worse - barren and unsustained in here."

He pounded his chest and looked earnestly at me, as if to say "I am serious". Still leaning forward he carried on, hushing me with his hands, but clearly desiring some non-verbal response.

"How bad could morale get? Bad. Because not only was diversity gone, it was apparently gone forever. Hope and trust in the system had died. You might think that disillusionment would creep up on a society unseen and unmentioned, and so it does in a *slightly* disillusioned society. But at this time, before the change, it had soaked in. It was news in itself. It was something people constantly agonised over: *'Why do we live like this?' 'What is the point?' 'Where are our values?'*

"You see when the behemoths take over, first of all it's the little annoyances, you cannot seem to get service from the people who used to care. Then you find you are the victim of sharp practice, then the minor extortions and finally all security and trust is gone as they have their will with impunity supported by colluding courts and bailiffs. At that point you realise that the authorities and peoples' representatives are also beholden or in cahoots. That our puny governments cannot stand up to the giants, that they are being pushed around as much as we are, and our leaders have abandoned the pursuit of fairness and happiness too. When a people realise that the bodies that were once benevolent and strong are rotten and weak and that the protectors have turned away leaving as consolation nothing but a plastic smiling face behind a two inch thick security window, all hope goes and like the slaves you have become, the only way to survive is through dumb, passive obedience. When, over the course of half a generation or a decade, all hope falls sick and dies, when humanity is starved down to its bones, that is devastating to people. When people give up on each other because of divisive oppression above and around them, that is when you know."

He paused. To recover energy I supposed. In any case I did not think I needed to ask the question.

"That is when you know that it has gone too far. That is how bad it can get. As bad as a person can stand."

He sat back and pinned a stare on me, and added "But no worse than that".

I was slightly frightened by this look. The journalist and critic in me switched off for a moment. Here, in the flesh, was some sense of the feelings of that time. But that look was beyond defiant and I was a little intimidated. I did not question his anticapitalist credentials after that, but I could not help thinking back to the sudden change of press. Who else had he intimidated and how?

Five

We sat back and sipped some warmed wine in silence for a moment.

"So what happened? How did you get involved in the movement that started to tackle that problem?"

"I was involved because of evolution – because of that realisation."

"The idea you got from trying to be a journalist?" I teased, mainly to lighten the atmosphere.

"Ah ha. You won't let that go will you." I was relieved he was grinning, but he continued in earnest. "But what is important is that evolution was the perfect answer."

" 'Evolution is revolution?' " I offered.

"If you like. I never really liked that slogan. We all wanted a revolution in philosophy, in people's world view, of course. Understanding the evolution did that alright. An ideology was emerging. Before that it seemed the only ideology was the neoliberal philosophy that excused a savage and domineering capitalism. But that ideology had already walked right into a trap.

"In the war of philosophies between change and status quo, the armies of the incumbent had seemed better equipped and in possession of the higher ground. Then we noticed, that in constantly pushing us back, forcing us to fight for our lives just to gain an inch of concessions for some tiny crumb of social justice or human right, we noticed that their entire army had wondered into......well, a kind of swamp. On the brink of our defeat, like a divine intervention, we saw that we had been regarding the Goliath down a telescope, and with the naked eye he was exposed."

"A swamp?"

"Yes, why not? Their ideology had wondered into something very boggy, put it like that. We could not have won such a decisive battle if it had not. You see the free-market religion, as it was then, worshiped evolution. They thought of it as a science that backed up their ideology. I think the survival of the fittest idea appeals to the callous end of politics and economics, but in any case, they genuinely believed that the theories of evolution proved the case for the brutish system we had. It was often cited when people complained about their rights or resources being destroyed by some horrendous oppressor. When the little guy was put out of business or locked up, or bankrupted or starved of opportunity, or just starved, if the most tiny restraint

Beyond Survival of the Fattest

applied to a rabid capitalist would have prevented the injustice, they would say – 'Ay yes. But it has to be this way. That's Darwinism'.

"They meant that the market was God and that we had to worship it because it worked through evolution which would ultimately work for the greater good. Whether they actually believed that, or if it was just self-interest talking, doesn't matter. The point is that by allying themselves with the evolution argument they were up to their knees in something sticky. And in the face of an explanation of the real evolutionary processes at play, they would sink further under the weight of the counter arguments and the long suffering people, would seize their opportunity."

"So you could fight back while they were stuck in the mud. How did you fight back exactly?"

"Well, years before, my university department had formalised the two economic populations conundrum and ran simulations proving the need for the separation of the economies of folks and firms. Portunism could start when the more political in the movement took the ideas and turned them into a way forward – genuinely realisable solutions to a problem that was now becoming crystal clear. Yes, we fought back. Ideologically speaking, we burst the revelation over their heads and while they sank we charged in and hacked off the giant's head while the army of neoliberalism floundered around it."

"But that doesn't really explain anything, does

45

it? What does it mean in practical terms? What did you and your colleagues actually do?"

He thought for a moment.

"We argued better and with one voice. We had the better economics and ideology now. We were able to explain and predict many of the problems of the free-market from an enlightened view point – the evolutionary perspective. Capitalism's relative success, just like all evolving systems, was due to having a diverse population, competition between members of that population and a means of storing and transferring success from generation to generation. That exceptional power to find the most creative, efficient and valuable solutions is due to those three things – diversity, competition, copying – just as it is in nature. This was the intelligent version of the neoliberal's 'The free-market is Darwinism. It's survival of the fittest, mate. Deal with it!' And exposing the actual evolution happening made the awful flaw in the old economics self-evident."

"It was so self-evident that the initially hostile press suddenly came round to your side?"

"I don't follow."

"Was it at that time that the hostility of the press towards you started to wane?"

"I think we just broke out of one of the Social Silences. Up until that point the scientific literature in evolutionary economics - from Hayek to Witt to Silverberg - either deliberately denied that any formal evolutionary analysis was possible, or, if it did allow it, would always start with an evolutionary model that was successful. No help at all in modelling a failing system. No one wanted to write the evolutionary model that didn't work. It was easy, as well, to overlook the population of people altogether. That was symptomatic of the big business culture."

This seemed evasive. I wondered if they had succeeded only with invisible backers in a grand behind-the-scenes compromise.

"That does not explain why politicised writers at papers, whose owners had a strong vested interest, suddenly went soft on you."

"Oh I see. Well, no. Many large industries were worryingly influential before the Change, but not the media. They were a push-over given a little organisation. I knew enough about it from my earlier aborted career."

"Did you know the right people too?"

"No. Not at all. It was all a house of cards waiting to fall anyway. We just insisted on the application of some of Portunism in those businesses."

"Insisted?"

"The media was not the trouble once we got organised. That is not important. The point is that our model stood up to scrutiny, even economists ultimately had to agree with the conclusion which was…"

He took a breath evening the pace and expecting me to forget my line of questioning.

"Which was that, although a good system is a population of healthy competing firms, that is not what we had at all. We had two populations mixed up together – people and firms. People, or more properly people's job positions, if rewarded in a skewed way, will evolve a system that is twisted and lop-sided. You can model and predict how that lop-sidedness will result in a weird species of chevrons which results in a sort of cancerous gigantism, and we did. But every scientist and mathematician in computational evolution could see that having the two populations the way they were, spiralling together in a dangerous feedback, was not a healthy thing."

"Was there real consensus academically, at that time? That is not what I have read."

"Not everywhere, but mostly. In the computational world, yes, totally and almost instantly. It was undeniable you see, because we used evolution to solve problems all the time. You know, understanding chemical reactions, designing aircraft, siting power stations - all sorts of scientific and engineering problems. And we would never, ever, use multiple populations in science the way we had them in our economics. Actually in the computer, making evolution work usefully can be very tricky. Things easily get out of control. Here we had two populations dependent on each other's success. No equilibrium could possibly be found. Some sort of runaway affect is inevitable in such a configuration and it was clear that in the real capitalist world the runaway affect was choking us to death."

"So you won the intellectual argument for Portunism and left the neoliberals in a swamp with their heads hacked off?" I said. He laughed.

"Let's be very clear. No one in my field had any desire for revenge against any individuals. It was the incomplete philosophy, the system and the amoral corporations it created we were angry with. At first we were just compelled to defeat the mistaken ideas."

It was getting late and I thought the conversation would have more clarity on another visit so I ended the session soon after that, still not knowing how he had changed the mind of the media. The phrase 'a push over given a little organisation' stuck with me.

Jose Manic

Part 2. Why bees don't eat trees

Capitalism: Where did it go right?

Long before becoming tainted, around 250 years ago, free-market capitalism's unique sales message started promisingly. It was the need for freedom of competition and choice that neoliberalism's super-hero, Adam Smith, was so keen on in the early years.

Professor Smith is not your conventional type of super-hero. Although, you might think so, based on the faith capitalism's enthusiasts put in him. It can be disappointing to learn that his 'Invisible Hand', first mentioned in The Theory of Moral Sentiments[1], is not the equivalent of Thor's Hammer or Captain America's Vibranium Shield (although, I concede that having an invisible hand could have all sorts of benefits). It is the recognition of an important effect seen in populations:

Given a large set of individuals focussed independently on their own needs, a group behaviour or effect can emerge that was never the intent of the individuals.

Somehow most of politics and business has missed the memo about more recent insights into this process,

Jose Manic

but for science and economics this very real effect has now been demystified and formalised. So that today we have theorems and maths for the phenomenon and we call it Emergent Behaviour.

Long before the maths was worked out, politicians and business owners who read Smith's later "Wealth of Nations", forged a majority view that this is precisely the spontaneous emergence that must underpin the free-market principles to make the new industrial capitalism irresistible. But as industrialisation and capitalism developed hand-in-invisible-hand, vested interests, armed with their catchy and reassuring 'free market' phrase, proceeded to do exactly what Adam Smith advised against; create monopolies, manipulate prices and contrive to force down workers' wages.

Of course, those abuses will not be stopped by a slogan such as "responsible capitalism". That is as absurd as trying to fix the system by rebranding 'free market' as 'fair market' or 'responsible market'. No amount of sloganisation will revitalise a brand if the product is no good to people. Instead, we can now use current knowledge of emergent behaviour, and its special case of evolution, to answer this question: Does the free-market principle work for us now?

Competition is essential for evolution and evolution is the most obvious and prevalent form of Emergence we see around us. The central argument of this book is that, by understanding evolution in economics, we can take control of the future, that evolution is fundamentally important to our understanding and our potential. Yet evolution in economics was not taken up by Smith and not seriously considered by other thinkers until the 20th century. Smith has a good excuse for the omission.

Professor Smith was already 86 and 19 years dead when Charles Darwin was born. So our first insights into emergent behaviour from Smith were developed in complete ignorance of natural selection and evolution. Yet under industrial capitalism we have seen the evolution of a greatly improved way of life in terms of health, security and comfort. The capitalism thriving under a free-market philosophy has delivered not just the power to monopolise and manipulate, but also the very solutions and technologies that would uplift most of the down-trodden masses. It seems free competition has simultaneously allowed exploitation and enabled liberation. The challenge we face today is far more testing than a rebranding exercise. It is the disentangling of the exploitative capitalism from the useful capitalism. And understanding its evolution is the key.

What is useful about free-market capitalism is also what is useful in computer evolution. It is what simple idealised free-market capitalism does best: search for better solutions in an optimal evolutionary way. Mathematically, it pursues a search strategy that works by trying combinations of possibilities using a form of parallel processing. With a population of many individuals - lots of little parallel processors - all trying to do a little better, by accident or design, some will discover improvements. If the good solutions are rewarded and copied they will survive and accumulate. And because of the parallel nature and persistence of the search, unimaginably unlikely and inspiring solutions are evolved. Based on what we know today, much of it derived from computer evolution, we can mathematically prove how awesome evolution is. But an everyday example will show evolution's importance to us.

Examples of successfully evolved solutions occur throughout history, of course - from the first amoeba, to the extraordinarily successful Tyrannosaurus Rex, or the equally awesome, but far less toothy, electric toaster.

In his book Adapt[2], Tim Harford describes the work of design eccentric Thomas Thwaites who tried to make an electric toaster by hand from natural materials.[3] Thwaites showed that even with nearly a year's effort this was practically impossible. His resultant machine looks more like an overambitious blancmange than a toaster. It is painful to use, burns the toast and is likely to set fire to your kitchen. Harford points out that this illustrates how 'adaptation' is the powerful force that has made complex and valuable solutions in our modern society common place. If the humble toaster can only come about by the evolutionary search through a complex web of technologies and supply chains, what of the really difficult problems society needs to solve?

I am not sure the term 'Adapt!' does the awesome power of evolution justice and I will stubbornly stick with 'evolution', but whatever you call it, it has found impressive solutions in advanced medicines, modern farming, humanising technologies and virtually every life-giving and technological advance we have seen. These are much more complex than the electric toaster and would be quite impossible to discover and organise without the searching power of evolution among a freely competing population of enterprises.

This provides us with a fundamental starting point and a reason to pursue our understanding of evolution in capitalism. The first of a series of theorems for what we will grandly call 'Symbiotic Economics' - is simply:

Freely competing enterprises are necessary to find valuable solutions for society.

So far this has nothing to do with the bees of the title of this part of the book.

The aim is to understand how capitalism has evolved to become dominated by huge global enterprises, with people suffering under massive inequalities, in an apparently callous, hierarchical and too-often domineering culture. To do this we must understand how globalisation, inequality, hierarchy, callousness and gigantism evolve. Tracking down the series of unfortunate events and accidents of human nature that have caused such strife will require us to look at our lives and businesses (and bees) in a new light and constantly ask why things did not evolve differently. The results of the investigation will yield more essential principles of symbiotic economics where the two populations of firms and folks live and evolve together in mutual co-dependence. We can gradually build up the true picture of how this relationship became a cold and abusive marriage and not the sweet harmony it first promised to be.

Jose Manic

Two populations in natural balance

So far we have been talking about the evolution of a single population competing and breeding and solving. That is the population of enterprises. In Adam Smith's studies enterprises were sometimes rich traders or organised businesses, but also often self-employed crofters, craftsmen and artisans. For example, when considering the competitive and economic forces on labour, Smith made no fundamental distinction between an employed individual or installed machinery.[4] Job-positions within industrial enterprises were a new thing and eighteenth century workers lacked even the simplest web sites to send them job bulletins.

Littlebelle refers to a population of folks. As it applies to evolution and competition, he is actually referring to the population of job-positions. Of course, job-positions play one of the lead roles in our concerns and discussions in economics today and no sensible economist, including or since Adam Smith, has denied the significance of job-positions. But when it comes to the principles of free competition – a principle that is essential for driving the evolution of our economy – something has been missed. That is the need to make a careful distinction between the competition between people for job-positions and the competition between enterprises that provide them.

Just like Smith the modern day capitalist has the regrettable and ultimately disastrous habit of assuming that the role of the free labour market is the same as the role of free competition between businesses. This book shows that they are not. And this is why Littlebelle insists that the foundation of Portunism is the acknowledgement that there are not one, but two evolving populations.

The state-of-the-art in systems of evolution, with more than one population, comes not from economics, but biology and computer science. In computer evolution individuals that make up a population are just numbers in the computer. Yet they have simple genes represented by strings of digits - similar to strings of nucleic acids - simple behaviour, a simple and very short lifespan and they usually both breed together and mutate. Despite being a simplification of real world evolution, evolutionary computation is successfully used in industry to design aircraft, develop electronics, configure power stations and solve a variety of other design and engineering problems just like Littlebelle described. Work in evolutionary computation and, more generally, in the science of emergent behaviour of populations of individuals, has led to a recent leap in the understanding of the processes of evolution.

Littlebelle claimed that artificial evolution in the computer would never use more than one population. This is partially correct. Some evolutionary algorithms have successfully used systems that mimic populations in predator-prey relationships and in many instances it is tempting to create an artificial environment for your population that coevolves with it.[5] But there are nearly always simpler and better solutions. In the cases where coevolution works with multiple populations there are invariably special conditions. For example, a smooth rate of evolution and an elastic relationship between fitnesses where one population pulling ahead always pulls the other along faster. Such carefully designed cases can indeed yield results in computer evolution.

Evolution in the living world is far more complex than this ideal. For one thing it is symbiotic - meaning that species have evolved to be highly reliant on each other. It is the same for the species of firms and folks. They are clearly reliant on each other, so evolution in our economic world is also symbiotic. Think again of the world of businesses and work. We have a population of competing firms but also a population of competing folks. The people need enterprises and the enterprises need people. But the needs of each partner in this marriage are quite different. Understanding how the co-dependence plays out is where our little pollen-collecting helpers will come in. In the following sections we will see how such a symbiotic relationship can evolve in an imaginary natural world – for better or for worse.

Powerful evolutionary pressures quickly become dangerous if they do not stay in balance. One species can easily start to dominate and drive out diversity, bringing evolution to a halt. That is definitely something to be avoided. We have all heard the mathematical extrapolation of what would happen if field mice, for example, were allowed to breed freely with no predators. We would literally be up to our thighs in field mice within about 21 months. Of course this does not happen because, as the population increases, other pressures come into play keeping the population down, not least the pressure of dwindling food supply. In the artificial evolution of capitalist economics it is these sorts of pressures that need to be balanced. It needs no imagination at all to picture the disaster that would ensue if, in the populations of firms and folks, one population started to dominate the other. We would be quickly up to our thighs in something - it would not be mice.

Part of the Portunist argument is that non-living evolution must be treated with care. These systems are not as sophisticated as life and we do not have millions of years to wait for them to balance themselves. The evolutionary system of capitalism requires some smart and deliberate balancing if it is not to become stuck and stagnant.

Fortunately the evolving examples in the living world can teach us a great deal. Unlike in the artificial world, two-population systems in biology are commonplace. In fact, around half the species in the natural world are parasites and nearly all are hosts for parasites. Is that what people working in enterprises are then, a parasitic symbiosis? We can next answer this question with that other question - an important and serious economics question.

Bees and their trees

So why don't bees eat trees?

It may not be a serious option for bees on earth to consider, but it is a valuable idea that when worked through helps to understand how modern capitalism has evolved and how it might be changed. This thought experiment requires us to imagine a natural world similar to that on earth but one in which nature, through evolution, has taken some slightly wrong turns. In this imagined world we are perfectly entitled to ask, what the devil is wrong with the bees on earth? Instead of waiting around for trees and flowers to dole out a few miserly micrograms of nectar once a year, if bees had a bit more gumption, and burrowed right into the tree to suck the energy from close to the source, they would surely fare much better. How would such a breed of bee prosper?

The new bee breed I will call the Parasite Bees. In our thought experiment, when the ancestor of the Parasite Bees – a primitive bumblebee, say - first came across pollen and nectar she saw it as an opportunity. She dived in and feasted. In this parallel world, a two stage adaptation was then started.

In stage 1, she would use her large mandibles to probe straight into the energy giving flesh. After all, many trees have an abundance of sugary sap, the closely related termites and ants can successfully live on trees and bees love making their home in trees. So why not make a meal of them too? If trees can be viewed as enterprises, then the bees are a bit like us people. They, like us, feed themselves on the surplus energy their host makes for reserves or for growth. This is a bit like us but far from the whole story in evolutionary terms.

In stage 2, the trees have to decide how to respond to the invasion. They have two choices. Either fight it, evolving defences against the invader to push them out, or turn a challenge into an opportunity and make use of the visitor. It will not surprise you to learn that in our parallel world the trees grasped the opportunity with both invisible hands.

Because of the huge challenge that pollination presents and its obvious importance to the success of the species, the trees decided it was better to have bees around than not. In our age and natural world we are familiar with what a dearth of bees has on pollination. A bee hive in an orchard can collect 100 pounds of pollen in a year. That is a lot of fertilisation, and all motivated by trees' insatiable desire to reproduce. Trees really need bees around.

So for trees in any world, keeping the bees sweet is a no-brainer. And since trees have no brains, keeping the intelligent and well organised little beasts around may be a smart thing to do for other reasons too – as we will see later. Therefore in this parallel world, let us say that the trees not only evolved to tolerate the trunk burrowing bee, but also started to accommodate them on their own terms, supplying food inside the tree trunk itself. In this way the bees would not have to nibble away at growing shoots. Let us say that the trees also evolved to regulate the flow of this special bee sap so that in hard times, if the cost-benefit of having so many bees tips the wrong way they could turn off the sap tap.

And so, through evolution, a happy partnership is

achieved. It is a bit tough for the bees if the nectar stops flowing but hopefully they will have honey reserves to fall back on or, in the worst case, they can try to find another host. Evolution has now taken the bee breed from the humble bumblebee to Parasite Bees to "Partner Bees".

So this would be a simple two population evolutionary solution. The tree has evolved to provide food and shelter and turned the invaders into something useful that is beyond parasitic. The Partner Bee, like most parasites, will inevitably evolve to become exclusively reliant on the bee sap and will happily pollenate vast areas of forest during its quest for pollen (say, because it makes ideal bee baby food as it does for bumblebees) allowing the tree to get on with the serious business of the large scale manufacture of wood and greenery and oxygen and other good things that it likes to pursue.

For a moment let us pause to think of those first Partner Bees and what has just happened to them. Since the tree saw an opportunity and adapted to its new little friends, the bee no longer has to travel so far. It lives right in its food source. In fact some of the worker bees never see the light of day. Food is provided for them and they live in the dark crawling about and digging out their new world in the trunk of a tree. In a short time these bees have had to adapt quickly to a dramatic change in their environment and in their changing fortunes, and they have developed specialist roles – mining for sap, for example. For a brief time these "Proletariat Bees" have no choice but to exist in an adaptive struggle to meet the needs of their new host and forge their new role in the world. The inevitability of the bee's rapid adaptation to the hosts' needs gives us the interesting corollary to our symbiotic economics:

Co-evolved symbiotes have to adapt to conditions within their host that would have been intolerable to their ancestors.

But back to the Partner Bees. Nature, with time on its side, has taken the initial unbalanced parasitic relationship and evolved a workable balance and something much more mutually beneficial.

Encouragingly, this is also the basis of the relationship between firms and folks. This should provide us with hope. For the neoliberalist it would be the end of the investigation. Everyone is competing, the market has found balance and every little hard-working worker bee can have her fill. But observation tells us that not everything in the garden is so rosy. Something does not quite fit. For example, why are the trees so big now that they span the globe? Why do we have some enormously fat bees and some struggling starving bees? And why do so many people still feel like the Proletariat Bee, toiling in a hostile environment to which they never quite seem to adapt?

Nevertheless, the two population balance is an excellent starting point for understanding the full ecology of our economics. From here we must investigate the large inequalities and hierarchies we see in our economics but never in nature.

Specialisation and being special

Trees in our world are fairly simple organisms and the bee has a simple role in the above example – to pollinate. Enterprises are far more complex and varied, as are the job roles they give their workers to do.

In the above story of the Partner Bees, the trees came first and later the bees got tree-involved. The trees existed and were established long before the bee discovered the pollen and nectar. This is not the same as the evolving world of enterprises and people because it is impossible to imagine, or even to legally construct, a business without people. Folks have a much more intimate relationship with firms than the Parasite Bees have with their trees, because they were there at the very start. This is what Littlebelle means when he says that the two populations are convolved.

So in our parallel world we have to make the first of a number of changes to the nature of trees to reflect the way they have coevolved with a creature that is far more intelligent and sophisticated than they.

We can predict that in the parallel world, a tree will have the need for a number of types of specialisation. Let us say, it needs the worker pollen-collectors, but also: the honey makers, the bread makers, the food storers, the child carers, the ventilators, the bouncers and the impregnators. I am not sure why the tree needs and has encouraged these roles in our parallel world, but these roles are dedicated functions and all happen to be jobs that real honeybees take up in our world (not names based on indie rock bands).

Throughout nature, in the wider ecosystem, we will see diverse and complex specialisations. These specialisations are divisions of labour (something Adam Smith was very keen on) that are necessary for the efficient operation of those ecosystems. What is unusual in our parallel world is that all of the different roles are taken up by the same species – what we must now call the Special Bees. Normally in biology, where timescales are much longer, evolution will cause such a divergence in roles that they become different species. In our economy, and in the complex forest of the parallel world, all the roles are fulfilled by basically the same species.

Perhaps surprisingly, in reality the roles in bee colonies actually have some 'social mobility'. They happen to compete less in the summer when the nectar is abundant and the main aim is steady, efficient production. But in the harsher winter, when there is fierce competition for resources, honeybee workers will compete for, and switch to, the more sought-after jobs. Our human species also competes, of course. This is one reason why the bee, with its discrete roles in the colony, is an excellent model for our thought experiment.

Back in the parallel world, let us say that each bee larva starts out with the potential to become any type of worker or drone (known in real ecology as 'castes' of bees) As they mature, the competition over the best roles will sort them out, with the roles most valuable to the tree being best rewarded and therefore most sought after.

This is a standard idealised free market system with diversity and competition for job-positions. For a scientific analysis of this system I will draw upon the animated film, Bee Movie. In this Disney world, young ordinary worker bees have the ambition to become pollen collectors in the same way that North American boys want to become fighter pilots or astronauts. And what is more, following the American dream, it is possible, if you have enough drive and enough cheeky persistence, to become whatever you want to be, regardless of your start and social position in life. This all sounds excellent.

However, if you look at the mechanics of such a competitive system a conundrum occurs. Let us say that the most valuable role is, indeed, pollen collector, making that job the best rewarded position. It then follows that it will tend to be the most sought after job. Now, if all bees start with the same potential it would make sense for all to start with the ambition of achieving the best position. Of course there is limited demand for pollen collectors, so some must fail to make the grade. That is fine, they can become bread makers and larva carers or whatever they choose second. But there is a problem.

A well working evolved colony or society is an optimal solution that will produce the ideal mix of all the available roles. Let us say that the best ratio of jobs for pollen-collector:bread-maker:larva-carer is 1:10:25. So that, for all those 36 bees there will be only one pollen collector required, 10 bread makers and 25 larva carers. Such appropriately distributed talents requires that some bees are more interested in becoming bread makers or larva carers right from the start. This would not happen if all the bees did in fact start out with the same potential. If they were behaving rationally they would all pursue the same role. This would be a big problem for the colony if the skills needed to fulfil those roles are at least partially acquired over time. If every bee starts with the same ambition many will not be developing the right mix of skills they will need in later life and those that end up in the bakery will sit and dream of blue sky and gaping vibrant flowers while the dough spoils.

The assumption that free market economics is required to make is that a natural diversity will solve this problem. Through diversity some bees are born with smaller wings than others, some may not have watched enough inspiring Disney movies and so are more easily discouraged, some just have a natural demeanour that suits them to menial tasks. But, observations of our current system clearly show how talent is not always directed so conveniently by the market. The problem has been exemplified by economist Ha-Joon Chang with the situation in South Korea where in 2003 four out of five of the 'top scoring university candidates' in the science stream, wanted to study medicine – many times exceeding the demand for doctors, while other science and engineering jobs were hardly getting a look in.

In another vivid example of the misdirected talents problem, 15 million U.S. residents hold at least a bachelor's degree in a science, technology, engineering or mathematics discipline (the so-called STEM subjects) but three-quarters of them, some 11.4 million people, work outside of STEM.[6] It is clear that many bright students are motivated to move into certain subject areas only to find that their many years of training are never put to use, resulting in millions of person-years of human talent being wasted pursuing ambitions that can never be fulfilled.

We suffer this problem largely to avoid the reverse problem. Which is that, if only 1 bee out of the 36 baby bees wants to be a pollen collector, 10 wannabe bee bread makers and 25 with a calling for larva care, then there would be no competition for jobs at all. The pollen collector could well turn out to be a dud, the bread makers complacent and, at the bee kindergarten, being devoid of any need to compete, the larva carers will organise some very dull sports days. This is the opposite problem to the misdirected talents problem and one which earlier capitalist systems often suffered from when class systems were too rigid to allow any mobility. Rather than being over-achieving, top-of-the-class dynamos of industry, the 19th Century European estate-owning pollen collector equivalent was too often a dissolute, inbred, cruel and narrow minded collector of rent. The rigid class system ensured there was no competing to become an aristocrat and this was a situation that industrial capitalism, following both world wars, took the opportunity to erode by introducing greater opportunity and social mobility – in affect reducing the rigid diversity of the population.

The inescapable conclusion from this is that, yes there can be role mobility within the colony, but for the society that requires specialised and varyingly valued roles, some individuals must set their sights lower than others. Some must decide from the outset that, no, the better rewarded jobs are not for them. For them the probability of achievement is not high enough to warrant having the ambition. This cause of diversity could be genetic – smaller wings – or it could be environmental – social discouragement. I suggest that our capitalist culture prefers a system of culturally induced discouragement. This is painfully practical because an environment that regulates opportunity by applying expedient levels of discrimination can be readily adjusted. Breeding smaller wings will take generations, whereas clipping wings by making the boundaries between strata of society impermeable, can be done in an instant. A simple government policy, institutional ruling or prejudicial culture will do it.

This process of obtaining an optimal level of diversity can be summarised in the second of our symbiotic economics conclusions:

Evolved solution networks will balance inequality of opportunity with inequality of reward.

This is why the Partner Bees' transformation into Special Bees is important to our understanding. They can efficiently fulfil specialist functions but that efficiency can be achieved either with high levels of equality of reward and opportunity, or low levels, or something in between. The point is that those inequalities balance each other out to achieve efficiency, opening up the possibility of an effective, yet highly unequal colony. We are all "Special", but for some that term may have very negative connotations.

We have shown so far that specialisation, which is inevitable in an evolving population and has many efficiency benefits, comes with its own risks. However, the above balancing act could be achieved either way. A balance is required but that need not be at high levels of inequality. What if there were low inequalities on both sides? It could be, for example, that in a basic free-market economy as prosperity increases the value of specialised roles tends to equalise, reducing the inequality of reward and therefore increasing opportunity and forming a harmonious system - more like Bee Movie than Battleship Potemkin. Unfortunately there is another pressure applied to our evolving economic systems, one Littlebelle made a great deal of, and one that ensures there is a very high level of inequality of reward.

Invention and hierarchy

Evolution works thanks to the building blocks of partial solutions.[7] It is not possible to invent from scratch a glow worm or a giraffe or a human being or an electric toaster. In life, partial solutions that are reusable across species, such as legs, eyes and lungs, had to be first discovered and then put together. Creatures and toasters are networks of such solutions and the clever partial solutions go right down to sub-cellular level. For example, all animals use tiny chemical power packs in their cells called mitochondria for transporting energy, and all electrical appliances use electricity and copper. These are partial solutions that were a hard earned step in the evolutionary process.

What is more, the layering of the solutions is crucial. Building up layers of partial solutions is the method that tends to work best where a complex solution needs to be searched for in the real world. In fact, mathematically it is the only way such a search for the solution could practically succeed.

Examples can be seen clearly in the manufactured world. Working upwards, a modern electric toaster will be made from basic metals of copper and silicon (one partial solution layer) collected into electronic components (another partial solution layer) then collections of components to perform specific functions such as power supply, perhaps circuit boards and major components in another layer, then finally the whole unit.

At each discovery of a partial solution a wonderful thing is happening – the whole is becoming more than the sum of its parts. The parts make something new. Mitochondria use fairly simple chemistry but the reactions as a whole create the new process of energy transportation. Energy transportation, with a few other clever methods, makes a living cell. Once a set of base components at one layer are found from which lots of things can be built, the organising force can ratchet up a layer and go about finding the next innovation. We can visualise this process as a network of Nodes of Invention. This is not just a convenient approach. The layering method is absolutely necessary to evolution and the need for Nodes of Invention is the reason just about everything in our man-made world is made up from layers upon layers of standard components.

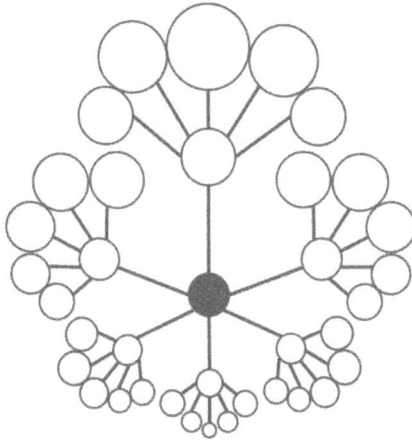

Figure 1. An optimal arrangement of job functions in a small enterprise. With the most valuable nodes on top, the network arranges itself with the ultimate objective and most senior node (filled) at the center.

An optimal business organisation with people and processes and equipment, then, should have the same Nodes of Invention - and it does. Individually, engineers may engineer or drivers collect and deliver or shop staff stock and stack and sell, but together they: design a new machine; form a logistics team; or provide groceries. At each point there is a Node of Invention and we tend to put a person in the position of that node; someone who can understand and coordinate the connection between the nodes below and the nodes above them. For example, between driving and a good delivery service or between shelf-stacking and a good shopping experience.

In Figure 1 we have a fairly typical small enterprise organised in a currently atypical way. In the diagram the job-position importance is arranged vertically, with biggest/most valuable at the top. This might be a non-hierarchical Architects practice, for example. In this example the centre node (solid circle) is the Practice

Manager. She is not as valuable as the Chief Architect at the top of the diagram, but even though the Chief Architect adds most value to the enterprise, he still reports to the Head of Architectural Design. That head, like all the other six heads, represents a Node of Invention that reports to the central Practice Manager. So if the top cluster of six nodes is the most valuable Architectural Design department, the other five departments going clockwise from 2 o'clock could be say, Project Management, Finance, Office Admin, and, increasing in value again (apologies to all those who work in Admin!) IT and Bid Management. Such departments and their relative importance make good sense to us at work and in this diagram they are arranged in the mathematically optimal order for an efficient organisation. This is the best way to arrange job-function Nodes of Invention. But this is humans we are talking about.

Humans have characteristics other than the ability to organise around a Node of Invention. For instance, humans have childhoods and instincts that make them interested in, and responsive to, authority. No bad thing you may think considering that everyone needs to work together with a degree of discipline, and I would basically agree. Also humans are not like components in an electric toaster. Those are soldered into position. We are not. We require motivation to do the job we are given, usually in the form of reward and usually the reward is heavily influenced by the human representing the Node of Invention – your boss. Finally, humans also have a tradition and history which means that they associate hierarchy in business with ownership of the business.

The net result of the human concerns of authority, motivation and ownership is that a particular type of network of Nodes of Invention will prevail. This is the hierarchical network. If you ask around today you will find that most people are amazed if you suggest that their boss is not automatically entitled to a share of the success of everyone 'beneath' them. Instead of a coordinator of function, as required for the optimal network, the boss's responsibilities have expanded to become mentor, parent, keeper, tamer and tax collector of all their loyal subjects. A new breed of bee will inevitably evolve in such circumstances. The Special Bees have turned into the Royalist Bees.

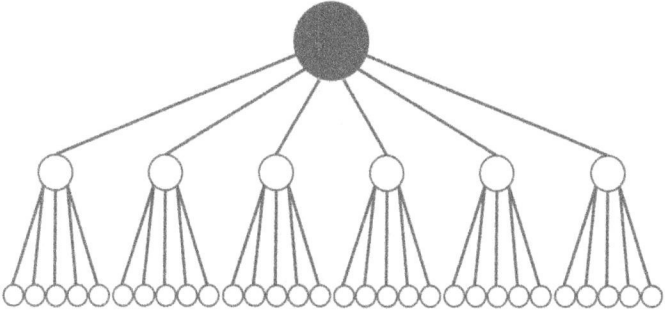

Figure 2. A sub-optimal arrangement of job functions in a small enterprise. With the most senior node on top, the network is hierarchical with more valuable job functions often subordinated.

Figure 2 is the same architects' practice, now organised hierarchically. The Chief Architect, at the top, is also likely to be owner, ultimate authority, supremo organiser and the 'Daddy' of the whole organisation. This is a more rigid structure and is suboptimal. For one thing it requires of architects, if their practice is to be successful, exceptional abilities in areas of expertise way outside their specialism. The result will inevitably be that only the few specially endowed architects reach the top of the tree, while the most talented and focussed architects are less successful.

Compared to what is needed according to the maths, these expansive responsibilities for a Node of Invention are unnecessary despite seeming very natural in our culture. We do not need to judge the process or try to fight human nature in order to understand the evolutionary pressures. But we must acknowledge the differences between what self-organising free competition can provide through evolution and how evolution, mixed with human nature, tends to structure our businesses. Understanding the difference between the evolutionary need for Nodes of Invention and the human tendency to hierarchy is vitally important when you look at the evolutionary pressure a firm will apply to individuals high up in its hierarchy.

This tendency is expressed in the proposed third theorem of symbiotic economics:

Hierarchies in the enterprise are the product of optimal evolution and suboptimal culture.

We are beginning to understand how our grossly unequal and hierarchical society could have evolved now. But I do not think a medium sized architect's practice like this, or any other such Royalist Bees' enterprise is dominating and grossly unequal, threatening the world's ecological and economic balance due to its fearsome scale. We need to continue the evolutionary journey to explain why our firms would become so overly stratified and so oversized.

Hierarchies and the capitalist caste system

We are so accustomed to authoritative hierarchies that it may surprise you to learn that bees in our world are not organised in a hierarchical way. Even the so called Queen Bee (the name we have given that egg-laying specialisation is telling in itself) has no real control over the colony. If anything, she is the servant of the worker bees who will kill and replace her as soon as her fertility drops. Back in our parallel world, if we create Royalist Bees and see what further pressures evolution applies to them, we should see the full implications of the human hierarchies. So, on the parallel world we will, for example, have pollen-collectors that are more valued and less numerous than the workers below them. Just like in Bee Movie, except now the pollen collectors are also endowed with authority over the other specialists.

To picture this, let us say that the worker bees need to be told where to put the eggs, when to feed the larva, how much honey to make etc, etc. And in the parallel world it is the more senior pollen collectors that are the creatures to tell them. How they know better than the workers in the centre of the hive when they are racing around outside is, metaphorically, a question that modern enterprises are constantly battling with in our real world. But that is not a subject for this book. The important point, and the consequence that dramatically changes the trajectory of the evolution of the enterprise, is that these extended roles now represent a risk for the tree.

What if a pollen collector does not perform well? Then the colony may suffer some of course. And what if a Larva Carer under performs, she may have a number of larva in her charge so this is bad too. But the pollen collector has 25 Larva Carers it is responsible for. If they are all given the wrong instructions that could be disastrous. In the hierarchically organised parallel bee world, the pollen collectors' performance represents a significant risk and there is only one possible evolutionary response to such a risk.

Increased risk puts the value of the bosses up. The colony must ensure that only the very best commanding pollen collectors are chosen. Therefore it must increase the intensity of competition for this role and in evolutionary terms, as well as in metaphor, this is done by increasing the reward. More generally, we can conclude that unbalanced rewards are an optimal solution in a hierarchical organisation. In such a hierarchy, it is not just that top jobs are more fun or valuable, they are also more critically risky and therefore attract a disproportionately high level of reward.

Now recall the second of our symbiotic economics conclusions: *Evolved solution networks will balance inequality of opportunity with inequality of reward.* It follows from this that, with increased differences in reward within a given enterprise, there must also be decreased opportunity in the wider solution network – our society. It also follows that, where there are extremely well rewarded positions, the optimal response for the system will be to deliberately place obstacles in the way of opportunity and social mobility. This is a must to compensate for high levels of differences in the motivational rewards of competing individuals and in the extreme case 'castes' will be formed.

With real world bees, as with humans, a caste is a group of distinguishable individuals who have very different and separate life paths from other groups. The honeybee we know on real Earth is very good at such segregation, with its castes of queen, drone and having numerous types of worker caste. In the colony in the parallel world the castes are needed to balance the high levels of inequality. If size of reward is proportional to hierarchical height, then castes will evolve to create the right balance of inequality of opportunity. The fourth theorem for symbiotic economics is:

An evolved environment that is hierarchically organised has exaggerated castes of workers.

We can now see what will happen due to the need for: specialisation; the human tendency to hierarchy; and the riskiness of bosses forcing up boss-rewards. The evolution of enterprises will create diverging strata of specialist roles and lifestyles. In the extreme case, or if the forces are not checked, we will have castes forming. This is a worrying forecast, but at least it does not predict that oppression and gigantism will evolve. Right?

Jose Manic

Gall Wasp growth

Bees are probably the most intelligent of insects. Experiments have been performed with bees to test their performance in finding the shortest routes around multiple points to visit - the so-called 'travelling salesman problem'. In this special mathematical task, which is handy for plotting a route around flowers but has no known method for solving perfectly, bees, having brains the size of a pin head, will find the shortest route with a remarkably small number of tries – a performance comparable to the methods used by supercomputers for serious number crunching.[8]

Trees on the other hand are as thick as two short planks. They have no brains at all. They just grow without a single thought for anyone or anything. This is another area where our metaphor works well for modern capitalist firms. You might think that the firm you work for does some daft things, but a firm without people, if such a thing were possible, would be as dumb as a stump. For our parallel world to reflect modern capitalism the bees of the upper caste must do more than collect pollen and direct the workers. Two more important characteristics do the final piece of damage.

Let us adjust the nature of the parallel world again. We are entitled to change an invented world, and we are now going to add environmental forces to create a world where trees without bees are as useless as firms without folks.

If you were to travel to this version of the parallel planet you would experience a very strange environment. Real Earth has a single sun about which it musically spins with a simple 4-4 rhythm to the seasons. Standing on the alien world you would see, let us say, seven 'suns' between which the planet meanders like a drunk at a barn dance. It follows some determinant path, but instead of the 1-2-3-4-1 seasons we are accustomed to, it staggers through a bizarre 1-2-3-4-5-6-3-4-5-2-7-8-4-3-5-1-2-3-1series. Those eight seasons are as severe as they are botanically unpredictable and high winds have kept vegetation bonsaically dwarfed. But as if this were not bad enough, a weird geology has also resulted in thin soil with sparse and hard-to-find nutrients. All in all, this is a much tougher and less predictable environment for trees than in our natural world. So, in this environment, the trees are helplessly reliant on the bee colonies not just to pollinate but also to guide intelligent root growth.

The way the dumb trees cope is to employ the bees' tiny, clever minds in continual missions of reconnaissance to sniff out new areas for potential growth. The miniature scouts seek out the life-giving nutrients and water that the tree needs, whereupon on-looking associate bees swarm to the area, or convey in lines like their closely related cousins the ants, and inject, in the way of the earthly gall wasp, into the desperately searching roots the appropriate growth auxin to tell the tree where it needs to develop. In this beautifully symbiotic relationship the trees, by hosting the new breed of Controller Bees, can outcompete all other plants by utilising an intelligence that is impossible with just dumb botany.

What are the evolutionary consequences of this?

Actually the consequences of the Controller Bees are not too severe so far. If you were thinking this would necessarily evolve into a system with rampant growth you were wrong. In this evolutionary symbiosis there may now be a great emphasis on growth, but still the trees will prefer their natural size. There is no indication that the Controller Bees would encourage the tree to break through that optimum. After all, if the tree host became too big to be healthy that would put the colony of bees in jeopardy too. Likewise, the trees are not dinosaurs. They gain no competitive advantage from being huge. So the evolutionary pressures that restrict growth will remain intact to ensure the Controller Bee provides a crucial, yet constrained, contribution to the tree-bee partnership.

This reasonably balanced state of affairs will persist as long as the regulating evolutionary forces are balanced. For real world bees this is achieved by sharing rewards across the colony. This will change dramatically in the parallel world.

Jose Manic

Independence and domination

The great discovery of free-market economics was that when individuals follow simple selfish motivation, behaviour can emerge which is good for the whole and all prosper.[9] And this is true. We know this because it is also a key principle of evolution and the theory has stood up to analysis, modelling and, to a large extent, is supported by observation of our economic systems of the last 200 years. But the theory of positive behaviour spontaneously emerging from the group requires a commonality of characteristics across the individuals, whereas we have seen how human beings are constantly pulling against commonality. We introduce strata, hierarchies, inequalities and castes that oppose the way complex solutions would ideally organise. So far there has persisted one overriding force that has been the gravity necessary to maintain the evolving population. The cohesive force of sharing rewards across the colony needs to be investigated a little more closely to see how it will bear up.

Every living individual is most interested in seeing their own genes passed on. For all evolving life, this is the ultimate reward. Bees are no different. For them it is about reproduction - not the honey or the flying privileges. What bees really want is to pass on lots of their own genes to many successful bee larvae.

In a bee colony the success of the genetic code of an individual depends on the whole colony. Over generations, the genetic code is shared across the whole group via a complex system of related families with shared and half-shared genes. This is why all workers are female, all the drones are male and there is a queen but no king. The sharing of the genetic reward is so intertwined that scientists often view the bee colony as a single superorganism.

The way a colony of bees on earth shares its gene pool around individuals is surprisingly smart and is clearly a deliberate tactic by evolution. But the point is that the genes are shared, so the success of the colony equals success for the individual. It means the focus of each individual can be to see the colony prosper. Perhaps this is why we regard bees with such affection. We know that the foragers will strive for a good harvest of pollen, the larva carers will feed the young and the guards will protect them all - even sacrificing their own life if necessary. It is all for the good of the colony. In genetic terms, this is the very definition of altruism and is very like the behaviour we value most in our own cohesive communities and families. But the same sort of constructive altruism is not reflected in our artificially evolved capitalism however.

The reward system for the upper castes, or indeed any caste, in the modern enterprise is based on personal reward. It is usually the case that the firm is not entirely made up from a family or clan. Employees are, thankfully, generally free to leave. This does not necessarily make individuals extra-selfish but it does mean that their rewards are independent from other individuals in the firm. If I am an upper caste individual this allows me the freedom to pursue maximum rewards for myself. Obviously, it would be irrational to put my employer host at risk - unless I have another job lined up of course. Also, with the very highest castes in business, the success of the business will often be closely related, through direct remuneration and through reputation, to their personal success - although this is little comfort to the lower, more expendable castes. Nevertheless, in capitalist enterprises of today, it means that the altruism of the earthly bee is absent. We have the castes but not the cohesion of reward between castes. For equality of opportunity this is bad news, but the real problem is the effect on evolution and the advent of the Selfish Bees - the next stage in the evolution of our parallel world ecology.

Selfish Bees evolve when, like in modern capitalist enterprises, the cohesion of the colony is broken due to independent rewards. It turns out that the bees on our strange planet are not as family orientated as our honeybees on Earth as they never quite perfected the system of shared reward – the even distribution of genetic material. It means the drones developed a female version and went off and bred with each other, the honeybees added a male version and did similar, as did all the other castes. Even the queen diverged from the colony gene pool and became her own royal species. Now they no longer work for each other but solely for their own caste – or even just their happy selfish pairing. They are still social and reliant on a colony being present, just as a parasite is usually interested in keeping its host alive, but if the rewards are not shared the evolutionary forces apply in a dangerous way to the upper controlling castes.

Those top level reconnaissance bees may still be reliant on the other castes of cell makers and bread makers, but the crucial difference lies in how the tree sees it. Now the tree is not so interested in the whole colony. Why would it be? The host will adapt itself to ensure that the controlling boss is the one most rewarded and, naturally enough, that controller bee will adapt to be even more controlling. With the full force of evolution directed at the top controlling castes, its reconnaissance missions will become more searching and more intelligent, its waggle dances back at the hive more elaborate and communicative, and the auxins they inject into tree roots and shoots will become more potent and more frequent.

What of the other castes in this once-cohesive colony? These castes, evolving under their own rewards, will increasingly favour the purpose of supporting the Selfish Bees simply because their host does. If they do not back up the boss then their value to the tree would be seriously diminished and, evolutionarily speaking, they could even, if they had ears or could be thrown, be thrown out of the tree on their ears. So they will adapt to find the pollen that is the best supply of fuel for reconnaissance, they will provide sap-honey close to the routes of their masters' routes and they may even adapt, albeit against their natural instincts, to expend greater effort nursing the Selfish Bees' larva than they can their own. In short, the Selfish Bee, due to its pivotal position and not due to its overall value to the solution or colony, will become dominant over the lower castes.

This leads to our fifth theorem for symbiotic economics:

Rewarding independently across castes leads to dominating upper echelons.

Selfish Bee is not a single species. The castes that formed the colony of Selfish Bee's ancestors have evolved to become species of their own since they no longer swap genetic material with each other. The species we need to focus on now, to understand how our capitalist system has evolved, is the controlling and selfish bee species which we will call, for obvious reasons, the Greedy Bees.

These highly adapted and influential Greedy Bees are in charge of where and when and how much the tree grows. Its rewards are independent - not shared. And, as a high risk node, tends to be rewarded in proportion to what the host can afford. In the short term, at least, it will favour growth. The Greedy Bees that achieve growth will be successful and, if left unchecked, the consequential forces can provide a miraculous new type of organism.

Jose Manic

From greedy to gargantuan

Bumblebees on earth form colonies of a few hundred individuals. Evolution has determined that this is a good size for a colony. Much larger and the nest could be difficult to keep cool and safe. Much smaller and it may struggle to make sufficient quantities of cells for the larva and honey that will keep it through the winter.

This is true of enterprises too. It will depend on the trade the enterprise is involved in, but there is a large body of evidence demonstrating that enterprises too have an optimal size.[10] Unfortunately, putting upper castes in control of enterprise growth, combined with their independent reward mechanism, is an evolutionary pressure that can easily break through the bounds of that optimal size. We can see what happens when, next, we apply the final characteristic to our parallel world ecosystem.

Imagine if one day, through some process of random search such as mutation, a tree in the parallel world finds that not only can it put out roots, but also parasitic suckers. What if it discovers and uses that new-found parasitic ability to find other trees through which it can get energy and nutrients? That could be a very successful tree and a very happy ambitious little Greedy Bee.

In enterprises in our current capitalism this process

has been going on for about 200 years. It is called Mergers and Acquisitions. Given what we know about optimal sizes of enterprises and what economists have been saying for decades about managers wanting growth and owners needing profit, we can see that it is the Greedy Bees that are driving the expansion that forms very large enterprises. Because evolution works much faster in the artificial world of economies than it does in the natural world, we have not noticed the terrible dangers in this process until now. The privileged Greedy Bee, due to overwhelming forces and new opportunities with parasitic trees, is evolving into the monstrous and ultimately self-destructive Almighty Bee.

Let us take a walk around the parallel world forest a few hundred thousand years after the tree first discovered those parasitic powers. The Controller Bees have now evolved to look for, not nutrients from the ground, but other trees to feed off. The trees' suckers have become far better at transferring the life-giving sap from one tree to another, so that now an Almighty Tree has emerged atop a mountain of trees. Coming across such an extended organism in the forest would be an awesome sight.

Descending the rim of a dank crater you would be vaguely aware that you have strayed onto the edge of a new kind of superorganism. Overhead the trees stretch into a darkening sky. They have nothing green to offer except a distant canopy. The structure is spindly, reduced to the purpose of transmitting energy from its bushy top to somewhere way above where a trailing tangle of lianas lead upwards. Just within reach of your straining eyes are areas of thicker growth – teaming galls induced by insects which plug into the start of a vastly superior structure that dwarfs even the first lofty trees. Its trunk is ahead and is as thick as a bus. The construction towers above with tentacles pumping liquid fodder upwards. But way above this looms the Almighty Tree. The base of that beast can be discerned in clinging fog ahead, as wide as a whale and with a knot of buttressing like an exploded cathedral, shrouded by a slate grey cloud of humming insects, like a battle just lost.

Out of sight but ever present, threatening as a hammer, at the top of the structure, the central monster is a bulging growth the size of a house – the home of the lethal head colony. In here, suspended in a mesh of regurgitated matter and oozing liquid latex, is the world's largest parasite. The ballooning Almighty Bee queen, all around preened by an army of dumb sightless roaches, is a bloated maggot hanging pulsating, hooked-up - at one end pumping eggs to an unceasing trail of audible insect legs, at the other a gaping hole sucking up the spew of a teaming swarm.

On the other hand, it might be rather unpleasant.

It is impossible to tell with evolution exactly how things will turn out. But we do know that such a cancerous evolutionary system will get too big and too dangerous and will try to take over the forest.

We have defined two populations - one of trees acting as hosts and one of castes of bees. We have found that, due to history and some unfortunate human-like instincts, that they will evolve the ability to create larger and larger networks of organisms. This is an ability they are destined to pursue to the nth degree as the prevailing and undiminishing evolutionary pressure on them is due to personal reward of the species of controlling bees that drive unending growth. It is no wonder that the forest floor is in shadow. Once the dominating castes discover their potential for unlimited growth a dark future is fated.

Long before organisms evolve to become larger or more dominating than their environment can withstand they are large enough to cause problems for evolution. A lack of diversity is inevitable when a few super-species dominate. And when those dominants are so reduced in number that the diversity is lost from their own population the chance of evolving new solutions will be reduced to zero. Failure to actively search for new ideas or solutions is stagnation. The absence of the living vitality of competition and innovation is death.

The scale and inevitability of the boundlessly growing organisms and the resultant demise of evolution is summarised in our sixth and final theorem for symbiotic economics:

Dominating castes will create gigantism and stagnation in a finite world.

Beyond Survival of the Fattest

Jose Manic

Part 3. Interviewing Dystopia (concluding)

Six

At this point the editor remembered his own drink and put the papers down. Looking around for his glass he noticed how dark the study had become. His beloved books above and to the sides of the fireplace were now crossed with shadows and behind a thin dark blue skin. As the whiskey filtered through him and he returned to the message under the reading lamp, he felt as if he really were floating through time. And then there was the journalist again, in bright summer-evening sunlight.

Further research revealed no new facts, just more suspicions. Mostly I was wondering whether the power that he and his colleagues had attributed to themselves to affect the course of the system, was even possible. Some of his claims seemed deluded. Anyway, I realised that the best source of information would be sitting right in front of me soon enough. And so to the final session, at the same cottage, in the abating summer weather.

"So I know you would rather not talk about

your inspiration for Portunism, for some reason." I was reading my notes on the table and moved some of my hair to look up at him. A smile. "How did the Portunist policies develop? You said there were major challenges."

"Indeed. Once the political groups discovered the idea, many liked it of course, but there was no consensus on a cure and not even agreement that the disease was curable. I suppose Portunism itself adapted, evolved, to meet the various demands and concerns. We also got very lucky. But when you are in darkness and the light at the end of the tunnel appears, you start to find your way and, with a little faith, luck will come."

"But is Portunism really engineered economics, like you have claimed, or just opportunistic politics?"

"I am not sure I fully understand the question, but it was, still is, based on engineered economics. It was brought about through politics, I suppose. I am not sure you could call it opportunistic. We had to split the populations. That was clear. The proof for that was my role. How to do it was for the real economists and the political."

"Okay, but you cannot get out of it that easily, Professor. You were at the heart of the movement that designed the roadmap for change. You were not just sitting in the background twiddling your thumbs in the early years. Do you still claim that you and your group actually engineered a change?"

"Sure. I can answer that one. Yes, there were

major challenges that looked unsurmountable at first. You see, if you take the three required ingredients to evolution – diversity, competition and inheritance – it was competition that was entangled between the two populations of firms and folks. That is what had to be deconvolved. We designed a way of separating the reward systems of folks and firms."

"How could a fledgling economic movement do that?"

"Before the change it was not the case that if an excellent worker wanted just rewards they would go to the most successful firm. They could work at an unsuccessful firm – a bank making huge losses, for example – and be rewarded handsomely. That is not a good fitness measure for the individual's work. Okay it rewards ability, but that talent can be wasted on a non-productive, valueless endeavour. The policy of strictly separating the populations by actually creating two currencies would be the key to making the change possible..."

"Taming the media, was that a policy too? You still have not told me how it is possible to change one industry let alone an entire economic system."

"Okay, I will explain. The newspaper industry is a good example for applying Portunism because that is an interesting illustration of how to dissolve businesses that are too big and too powerful."

"But how could you *induce* them to apply anything?"

"That is a different question."

Jose Manic

"Nevertheless, that is the question I have."

"Very well, it was like this. The media followed the daily nationals and, as you say, those papers were politicised, but they were also greatly weakened by online and citizen journalism. Their financial situation left them wide open to direct action from perfectly conventional consumer pressure. You see, they all relied on advertising for the vast proportion of their revenue and media advertising relies on minor changes in behaviour from those that receive it. Of course, those minor changes in reader behaviour can amount to a lot if there a million readers, but if you have fifty thousand ready and willing to *dramatically* change their behaviour – say by completely boycotting the supermarkets that advertise in a targeted paper – that far outweighs the normal benefits of advertising. The advertising agency will pull out and, if that is repeated, no paper can survive. With that sort of direct action and a little organisation, the power goes back to the people. That was our inducement and we used it. There were plenty of journos already sympathetic, but they couldn't get a look in. We changed that."

"But you would have to blackmail the papers over every issue."

"Not quite. But at first it was a fight, sure. We were having to engineer change all the time. But it became easier. You see there is nothing wrong with having a large national paper or any other far reaching product. It is having total control of it in one place that is the problem. Nationals survive today but they are not the pyramids they once were. The survivors are those that adapted to a break-up, that are in touch with their readership, that can compete for exclusive access to stories from excellent content providers and can gain the loyalty of the print shops. Like nearly all industry, they have gone from lumbering industrial giants run by egomaniacs to effective networked federations that produce a valued product. Not surprisingly, with central control gone, excessive bias and misinformation went too."

*

That explanation came as some relief and I confess that the technical summary that followed made me see things in a new light too. Until I had heard it from one of the primary architects I had not appreciated how, prior to the restrictions they had added, businesses were at total liberty to redirect any corporate profit to favoured employees. I had wrongly assumed that some form of restraint was natural and would have been present even before the Change. But I continued to confront what I saw as a too partial account of his own motivation.

"And the change itself, the conversion of industries to a new economic model, was that what you would call 'engineering change' too? Or was it actually just dumb luck that it happened at that time?"

"It *required* some luck. We could not have done it without the key economic and technological advances at the time, but different plans were worked on and one survived. I used to teach it as 'SLIM'. You know - we had to 'SLIM fat capitalism' - to Separate currencies, Limit wage ratios...."

I interrupted – "...Yes I know what SLIM stands for: Internalise the peoples' economy; Mutualise businesses. Very clever I am sure. But without that exceptional luck, was the plan worth anything at all?"

"SLIM was successful because it was a tool with which people could implement Portunism by whatever means they needed to. It broke from the traditional left and right, it was not totalitarian or democratic, radical or gradualist. No, I have got that wrong. It was radical, but at the same time got us over the old gradualist versus revolutionary debate. Here was a cause that a city or region or government could commit to immediately, without delay, with positive uncompromised steps that could also be gradually stepped up. The 'L' for limiting the inequalities of wages within a firm could be implemented at any level over any time scale, but at whatever the percentage of average salaries the tax penalty was set, it was a positive affirmation that unrestrained wage ratios were not going to be tolerated by the people - an acknowledgement that the cost of deformed rewards was arrested development and dysfunctional markets. The theory did not say how much taxes should go up for excessive wage ratios, but it was unequivocal that there would be some penalty. That alone was a strong enough message to start to give people hope of justice and progress again."

"Very good. And Mutualisation, as a worker's right to gradual ownership of their employing firm in lieu of their right to limited wage ratios, could be done equally gradually, right?

"Absolutely."

"Or devastatingly rapidly and severely?"

The Editor stopped and looked around the room. Something was there in his head – a vestigial memory or thought, not quite déjà vu, something more real. He read the line again "Mutualisation - a worker's right to gradual ownership of their employing firm in lieu of their right to limited wage ratios". Where had he heard that before?

He recalled vaguely that he was thinking about something similar on top of the news building that afternoon. A fleeting vision he had seen or read perhaps. For a moment the peak of an unacknowledged idea, associated with a feeling of hope and the promise of some peace, was surfacing from a slimy subconscious. But it was an ancient thought to him, confusingly filed in his mind amongst red flags and dangerous foreign enemies. He could not keep a grasp on the slippery tip of the idea and his mind slid back to editing out what the interviewee was saying.

Creating two separate currencies, limiting wage ratios, mutualising ownership - so it was Marxism, but within each enterprise, and with a new currency for the proletariat. How dull and backward he thought – "Don't these people known anything about free competition?"

He looked at the clock, feeling a little tired, then at the page numbers and then scanned the page ahead. Finally he resigned himself to the rest of 'Mutualise' and 'Internalise'. "Why not 'MISL'?" he thought brilliantly, with the benefit of another slug of whiskey.

"It was hardly ever 'devastating'. Some places, some nations, demanded quick justice it's true, but wherever the stability of the economic system itself was threatened authorities always reined back. These systems have to be given time to adjust. The whole point was not to throw the baby out with the bath water. With the system already as fragile as it was that would have been very dangerous. The point of Mutualisation was to preserve the real purpose of capitalism – the recycling of capital. If profit is the by-product of successful human endeavour, progress is only possible if that profit is reinvested into more endeavour. The Mutualism rules ensured that a pretence at ownership could not be used to skirt the Limit policy, while investors could still have the option of reducing the costs of labour in early years – just as they might forgo rewards to themselves. Gradual mutualisation over the course of a loyal worker's employment is the calculably fair alternative to enforcing limited wage ratios in the early stages of an investment in a company. It is just and it preserves the incentives of the owner investor."

He paused to see if I understood. I should have been quicker to jump in.

"That is the problem with most revolutions – they risk too much. Ours did not. New governments needed the levers to make the changes at a tolerable or optimal speed and we provided those levers with the SLIM framework."

"But you just took the credit for the natural move to protect the personal and consumer economy from the business economy - the I-for-Internalise. It was inevitable that given the creation of two Separate types of currency, one for folks and one for firms, that governments would want to influence the exchange rate between the two, force firms to declare as business-to-business or business-to-consumer, ensure businesses were legitimate enterprises and not just created to mask inequalities – all those policies that ensure the folks economy is kept distinct, that we take for granted now, were just inevitable progress surely? You just jumped on the band wagon and took the credit."

"I do not want to take the credit for anything"

– getting a little angry now. "I did not even ask for this interview. I am not claiming anything but telling you how it was. The Interning, the controlling of exchanges and the containment of the domains of business and human economics, was necessary then, as it is today, and it was planned. It is a necessity to preserve the Separation principle. Unless there is a gate between the folks' and firms' economies, businesses will always find a way to create those linchpin, over paid, top-of-the-pyramid positions. Yes, it was possible to engineer that. Thank God it was! The change that was already occurring naturally was the technological change that made that control possible."

"That is my point. You did not engineer the separation of currencies or anything else. It all happened by technological accident and a natural political momentum."

"I do not agree. But what difference does it make anyway?" - going up half an octave now. "Engineered or accident?"

"It makes all the difference in the world…" I had prepared this line of questioning. It was a growing political concern at the time. "If the greatest economic change that has occurred in the history of industrial capitalism happened because of a change in the direction of the wind, how do we know that it won't all just blow back again? The truth is, then as now, the people control nothing in a free-market capitalist system and you had become exactly what you did not want to be – not the great designer of a new future, but just another cold, deluded, ivory tower boffin observing and adopting the latest fad." Some tension seemed to leave him. He leant back again in his chair.

"I see. There has been a misunderstanding, perhaps." A sip of wine as he looked me up and down. "There are two things to explain then: Why that technological change was important, perfectly timed and fortuitous, but by no means essential for what we planned; and, how we know for sure that things will never, ever turn back."

Jose Manic

Seven

Back in the present the Editor put the sheets of paper down. He did not pick up his whiskey glass right away. He stared ahead and tried to make the shapes out in the darkened room. It was no good. He looked at his chair and legs and feet bathed in the reading light, the oval of light on the nearby bookshelf. There was no thunderclap or eureka moment but a growing feeling as his mind played over the terms and ideas and the mulling of what he thought was possible and what was not.

He drifted for such a time that it was a surprise to return again to the sunny future. There he found Dr Littlebelle was still talking in the evening sun light and the journalist still narrating.

"But I don't know why you are so hostile to the idea of us engineering the solution."

"There is no need to play the innocent Dr Littlebelle. Don't you think that you should have to defend your track record?"

"I don't understand. Why do you think there is

a need for controversy?"

I was not going to let him start interviewing me, so kept quiet.

"Ah, there is a need. You need some conflict or something new for your story? Of course. I am so conceited I was thinking my ramblings were still interesting in their own right. Oh dear." He looked around at the ground as if the words he needed had been spilled onto the floor. "I will have to disappoint you. You will get no angry ill-considered outburst." He was amused at himself I think.

"That's alright" I said, aware that he was eyeing me again.

"But you thought there was a revelation. That was it. You wanted to know about my inspiration all those years ago." He laughed suddenly and leant forward conspiratorially. "I'll tell you what. I'll give you the name – the journalist that gave me the inspiration for Portunism. It was quite an extraordinary thing. You might even know him."

I was shocked to silence at the breakthrough and he leant back again in his chair.

"But, tell me, is that a real doubt? Do people now really fear it might all fall back again?"

"I suppose so."

He was saddened by this. So we did a deal. I agreed to record and publish how they split the currencies to make all the SLIM policies possible and why it would not change back again. And the doctor vowed to tell me his secret. Like playground children we exchanged promises.

*

The machine was still sitting there, recording light flashing. But I took down the following with pen too.

"We were exceptionally lucky at the time we were winning the evolution argument. Not lucky to be winning it, it was a no-brainer, but lucky with the storm that was already brewing. Crymptocurrencies were fermenting and growing and Bitcoin was making quite an impact.

"Bitcoin. That was the first electronic money, the core cryptocurrency right?"

"Well, yes. Back then it was the only major cryptocurrency, but the derivatives from it were forming. A big political problem for Portunism had been how to turn one currency in a state into two. Some argued for revolution, boycotting banks, printing new folks money or focussing on the weakened countries in Europe – but as Bitcoin started to burn through the financial systems of the world it cleared our path."

"Did you know what was going to happen to national currencies?"

"To a point. We knew cryptocurrencies would succeed. It was unstoppably successful way before it was in everyday use. It had to be. The established banks and states had been trying to create real electronic cash for decades. Now this new thing took hold, some of the establishment tried to claim that it was just a passing thing, but it was the electronic cash system that worked - not fundamentally different from the ones they had tried to create themselves. And it was global and transacted almost for free with no banks. It was close to perfect. But the destructive force being unleashed was that people and firms could keep their money hidden from governments."

"And this lead to the tax crises. I know this much. That is why some people say the change was just an accident."

"No it wasn't. Because we knew it was coming, we could use it. We predicted the cryptocurrencies would rip up the old contract between state and people. The temptation was just too great for people you see. People of all types and political flavours could get paid electronically and hide the proceeds. Even the fiscally advanced societies in Europe were vulnerable, often more so than the struggling states. After all, they relied on huge tax revenues and employment taxes paid by businesses, not just deducted from salary. These things provided the motivation for businesses to join the cryptocurrency revolution too. First it was only those on the fringe, of course, but these things spread and this one spread like wild fire."

"You said it ripped up the contract?"

"Absolutely. A little bit of tax evadance here and there to many people didn't seem to matter, but when schools and hospitals are shutting, when the police struggle to keep going, when your country's borders are left undefended you know you have sleepwalked into a whole new nightmare. It was in everyone's interest to do a new deal. We had a design.

"We were the ones ready with the proposal. To maintain order it needed a new re-legitimised state to provide registered addresses – you know, the code numbers where you can pay and keep your electronic money - so its people and businesses could operate openly and freely and not in a black market. That was the only way. So what institutions, what ideology would people trust to do this?

"You see, now that the genie was out of the bottle, there was no way people would give up their new-found freedoms without a new deal. Only if the new state would deliver on a new economic promise, be committed to establishing greater equality through Portunism and maintaining freedoms would they sanction it. Then, with the simplest technology, that new authority could deliver on SLIM by adding the key ingredient preventing a cross-over between business and people transactions. By basic legislation and monitoring of the blockchain – you know, the public ledger of electronic transactions - to apply the Separation…"

He paused for breath. I think he could see I was getting a little lost.

"...You need monitoring to ensure that it is public information if and when business money becomes people money – exchanges through the port between folks and firms. If everyone can see the exchanges and everyone knows the rules on keeping those currencies separate it is almost self-enforcing. Two currencies, no oppressive state, a new system. It was beautiful."

I did not interrupt. I confess mainly because I really wanted that name.

"It was not immediate. Those simple policies of transparency could *almost* turn the one currency into two. But the astonishingly powerful change is that by just sign-posting the separation, as the interactions become more rare, they go on to diverge and evolve in their own ways and very quickly. Like two species evolving from one, they become so incompatible that the separation becomes natural and irreversible. Like two different animals – a peoples' cryptocurrency and a business cryptocurrency."

"That means you opportunistically took advantage of the tax crisis. Isn't that a bit cynical?"

"No, not at all. The tax economies in advanced societies had stumbled into a crisis. A new relationship had to be formed between state and the people. We did not decide what that relationship should be. We simply offered one alternative to the people - one they took up. The other options were a chaotic libertarian nightmare or an outright, and probably futile, attack by the state on people's new currency. Our offer cured a terrible 100 year disease and required no force. Just the harnessing of the force of evolution. And this is the other reason why the system will never fall back again."

I said nothing.

"The reason it will never fall back is that the new way is better. Not just for people, not just for evolution, but for human endeavour, for enterprise small and large too. When, having the Separation in place, the rest of the policies were introduced and the behemoths had to adjust by spinning out smaller companies, by paring down and teaming up and doing all those things that enterprising people and vital businesses are so good at to stay competitive. When they started doing that in one city or region or state and firms had to organise so everyone was working on the same endeavour and being rewarded proportionally, when one giant firm spun out the new supplier, when the local culture and natural human desire for status started to be more about the rewards of job satisfaction and creating value for your community and less about personal financial rewards, when that happened the dinosaur next door did not resist the change, it did not hire the overpriced teams that had been expelled.

"Instead, it also expelled its own waste, pared down, regurgitated the overpaid and in turn benefited from the spin-outs and freelancers as new suppliers. It did this not out of ideology but simply because the way with greater fairness, greater human motivation, increased diversity and greater efficiency, is more competitive. Those changes were adopted by the inheritance mechanisms of businesses not because anyone told them to do it, but because it works."

"How can we possibly know that?"

"The theory predicts exactly what happened, if you really want to see the models. It was so even before the Change. As an enterprise, it's about getting networks to work with you instead of against you. If the behemoth starts to go blind, as they often did in the old days, its internal network is a huge and entangling cost.[11] The eye requires surgery, drugs, years of treatment, pain and convalescence. Whereas, when the smaller, agile company in a cluster of businesses starts to lose its sight, it simply brings in new 'sight services'. The external network has 'external network value' instead of 'internal network cost'. Now they can get a new eye, with night vision, multi-spectral sensors and zoom lens. Do you see? No one wants the old dinosaurs back. They cannot compete with the new way, they never will, and we only suffered them because we knew no better."

That was it. His part of the deal was completed. The explanation that I was now committed to writing up, delivered. The interview in its entirety was not published until now. I summarised it at the time for our readership and the article came out quite well I think. I dutifully stressed the latter points on the new covenant with the people and why the change was forward and cannot go backward. Despite what they say about journalists, I at least, usually do stick to my promises.

After the interview we kept in touch and became quite close. I even wrote one or two pieces for him, but mostly I liked to listen to and debate his views on new developments. Some of them overly optimistic, perhaps, but what I liked was that he always wanted to explore what was possible.

Jose Manic

Eight

The Editor gave a full sigh but continued reading.

> That summer evening we continued talking for a
> while on more personal lines and he did give me the
> name which I can now reveal after all these years.
> Apparently, by some extraordinary means, this
> senior newspaper editor provided him with the
> initial inspiration for Portunism...

When the Editor saw his own name written on the
page he put the papers down and stared. He then shook
his head, crawled out of the cell in which he was sitting
and scrambled for the light. Stiff legged and wincing
from the brightness he hobbled to his briefcase.

"Where the hell is it?"

Eventually, found in a file marked 'Interns', was a
resume with *'Janus Littlebelle'* at the top. The Editor sat
down again, scanned over the document and reached for
the phone. He looked at the clock and around the room

while it rang. There seemed to be no light yet outside. A woman's voice answered.

"Is Jan there please? I need to speak to Jan"

Some whispering and then a man's voice.

"What you are trying to do is absolutely extraordinary" said the Editor.

"I'm sorry?" said the voice.

The Editor stood up. "We met this afternoon. You were in my office, telling me about your research and your plans. I didn't really know what you were talking about at the time."

"At the paper? Oh I see."

The voice thought it should try to sound enthusiastic and the Editor continued.

"What were you thinking? Did you think you could get the better of me? Do you know how long I have been in this business? When I started you were just a twinkle in the bloodshot, drink-glazed eye of the whore of Babylon. You came into my office and defiled my air with your poisonous, aborted embryo of a theory. You shrivel-brained, conniving psycho. I would not hire you. I only listened to you because I felt sorry for the family of retards that mistakenly spawned you. You will never work on my paper and while there is bile in my spleen I will see your vomiting crap is never printed or heard anywhere. You will not contact me again or send any more messages or give me any information on your measly life unless it is to give me the joyous news that it has ended. And when it does, I will be ready to meet you in hell where I will see you boil and burn with all the other fanatical vermin where your only relief will be me standing atop a pyramid of your daemons pissing on your head for all eternity. That's my vision for your future mate!"

The Editor crunched the phone down and crawled back into his seat. He regained his composure and thought for a moment. Then he returned to his briefcase and picked out a dictating machine.

"Company memo Sandra. Some of you may have heard of a hoax message that has circulated the office..."

The memo left instructions to destroy all copies, discount the nonsense perpetrated and not to discuss it. It also outlined serious penalties for failure to comply with the instructions including instant dismissal and potential legal action.

The editor thought that he should finish his whiskey. As he did so, he brooded on the despicable state of the world; the deviants, the radicals, intellectuals, bleeding hearts and layabouts that seemed to spring up everywhere. When finished, content with his long day's work, he went to bed and slept soundly until the new day.

*
* *
* *   * *

Part 4. Reversing Dystopia

What we can do

Finally, here is a conjecture, not a theorem:

The corrupted evolution of our economic systems can be fixed.

The processes that our theorems describe have an inevitability, but by counter balancing those forces we can call a halt to the excessive inequalities of opportunity and reverse the drift to a dominating and hierarchical culture. We can deny gigantic, growth-driven enterprises their ideal environment. Advantages will be more efficient capitalism, greater equality and a more humane culture.

Looking again at the inevitable rules that are played out in an economy of two evolving populations of businesses and people, we will see where to apply the brakes:

1. *Freely competing enterprises are necessary to find valuable solutions for society.*
2. *Evolved solution networks will balance inequality of opportunity with inequality of reward.*
3. *Hierarchies in the enterprise are the product of optimal evolution and suboptimal culture.*
4. *An evolved environment that is hierarchically*

organised has exaggerated castes of workers.

5. *Rewarding independently across castes leads to dominating upper echelons.*

6. *Dominating castes will create gigantism and stagnation in a finite world.*

The proposed framework to 'SLIM' fat capitalism, uses Separation and Internalisation of firms and folks economies and Limitation of wage ratios in the enterprise to counter the evolutionary pressures that increase inequalities and produce caste-stricken hierarchies in our organisations. This can control the effects of 2 and 3 – setting the balance of inequalities of opportunity and reward at a point of high equality and constraining hierarchies in business to levels that we can live with.

It reverses 4, 5 and 6 – by handing the bill for the costs of excessive hierarchies and dysfunctional economic evolution to those individuals and enterprises that currently exploit the inequalities and elevated hierarchies. These changes will ensure that 1 is preserved – healthy enterprises competing freely in an economy with a new purpose and an improved, more equal and sustainable culture.

Without such a solution enterprises will expand to the point of stagnation and ruin. The ability to endow the SLIM framework with policies of a suitably measured political flavour and an appropriate speed of execution, together with the principle of Mutualisation, ensure that the remedy can be controlled and is proportionate. Using again the economic model described for our parallel-world bees, we can see the recipe for this solution in more detail.

Firstly, prevent the bees from ever entering the tree. Bees should not be eating the food that the tree requires.

The danger that the two species will become evolutionarily embroiled is too great. Portunist versions of our trees would adapt by providing bee food in the form of a specialist currency called nectar – a watery sustaining drink that is nowhere near as potent as tree sap, but is perfect for an adapted little insect. To obtain the nectar they visit insect sized ports called flowers. It is essential that trees are prevented from letting bees feed directly off their own supply of wealth.

This is the Separation principle in the Portunism framework that Littlebelle spoke of in Part 3. Two currencies are needed – one for firms and one for folks. Businesses must not be allowed to divert their profit arbitrarily to favoured people. A more balanced system, as in natural earth's own ecology, is needed to control that.

Secondly, the rewards for all those in a colony must have an equalising force applied to counter the natural economically discriminating force due to differences in risk to the host. Without this, species are liable to diverge. Honeybees on our planet achieve this by sharing genetic material across the colony. With the reward of reproduction evenly distributed over the hive, every individual can play their part, castes are not overly exaggerated and a degree of unity is achieved.

This is the Limit principle. Rules are needed for enterprises to penalise large disparities in wages. If the job positions appear to require disproportionate rewards then there is something wrong with the size, organisation or viability of the business.

Thirdly, the bees must be protected from the trees' temptation to cheat the system. This is not necessary for honeybees in our world because they are already perfectly adapted to transacting with trees through the flower ports. But trying to reverse-adapt the Almighty Bee is a challenge of a different scale. In modern capitalism the creature with the know-how to burrow into and feed off trees already exists. It would not be possible to stop all bees and trees reverting to the old ways, but over time, by applying "Internment defences", the portunistic flower-feeding lifestyle will prevail and the bees and trees will evolve to make the most of it.

This is the Intern principle. Laws are needed to keep control of the currency exchanges when firms' currency is converted into folks' currency for payment of wages. And the use of a firm's currency or firm's privileges for backdoor rewards, such as bogus companies set up for the sole benefit of an individual, must be kept to a minimum through scrutiny, regulation and transparency.

Fourthly and finally, new saplings must be able to grow and prosper without violating the Limit Principle. The bee metaphor is not so apt as it is for S, L and I here, but the problem and the solution are straightforward enough. The problem is that the Limit principle may introduce an obligation to pay wages to staff that owners would not countenance – even for themselves. One of the achievements of capitalism is that it can allow the efficient recycling of capital. This means the profit from human endeavour in one area can be reapplied in another by an owner-investor. The equivalent for our bees would be that a sapling must be able to attract bees to pollinate it even before it is mature and strong enough to provide bees with nectar payments. The necessary solution, if you want a healthy crop of saplings, is that the young tree develops a relationship with bees whereby they are willing to work for less in the early years, in exchange for the promise of future reward – metaphorically, a hive of their own in the trunk when the tree is big and strong enough.

This is the Mutualise principle. A system is required where the owner-investor can be partially exempt from the Limit laws by offering workers the alternative of ramping ownership of the company. This can be done, for example, with a normal share ownership scheme. And the level of risk that the owner is taking versus the worker's commitment can be reflected in a discount rate – the standard financial method for comparing an upfront investment with future payments. This prescription for balancing and sharing risk and ownership is mathematically fair with the rate either set by the job market or by an authority.

These four changes are practical and achievable. In the next chapter we will come to specific policies that could be implemented today in any reasonably advanced economy. This puts paid to the argument that our neoliberal systems cannot be tinkered with, that it is somehow a natural order, that it is healthily competitive and that there are no alternatives without economic disaster. None of these views will stand up in the 21st century based on what we now know.

Jose Manic

Manchester Disunited

There will be further objections to change of course. Two obvious objections to this solution will be (1) that businesses cannot withstand being split and the policies would be economically damaging and (2) that, in any case "you cannot buck the market" – to slightly misquote Margaret Thatcher – meaning that people or the market will always find a way around efforts to control or confine unfettered capitalism. The theory shows this not to be the case and this is illustrated with an example of an enterprise which is firmly on the difficult end of the spectrum of Portunist suitability.

But first we will deal with the size objection – "Portunism will not work because having smaller businesses is risky and damaging to the economy".

Looking at the evidence, the idea that enterprises today are not too large and powerful is laughable. To balance any creeping concern that we could cause economic damage by slimming business, we should consider for a second what damage is already being inflicted with, for example: commodities companies that are too big to care about destroying the ecology of entire continents; or everyday consumer goods businesses too big and powerful to be charged tax; or the obvious example of banks that are too big to fail - literally taking us to the brink of complete economic meltdown. In any case, a healthy evolving and competing society excels at finding solutions. Apply a little creativity and imagination and you get a preview of the sort of solutions it may come up with. Even, as we shall see next, with the extreme example of a medium sized company with an entrenched culture of super-elitism, the economic alternative bears scrutiny.

Love it or loath it, a particular type of sporting enterprise provides the perfect example. Professional football clubs are particularly helpful in this analysis because of their top-heavy structure, their very clear aims and because, compared to other elitist and powerful businesses, they are far less likely to sue the author.

Manchester United Football Club should be a difficult example for Portunism for many reasons: its very high wage ratios; because it is a global concern competing internationally for very highly paid talent; because it also hires low paid workers for basic but essential functions; and because any loss in competitiveness will be immediately and painfully felt. At the same time, the clarity of its objective makes it very easy for us to understand the point of the enterprise and what success means to it. Clearly, it wants what its supporters want - to win matches and trophies in a way that entertains and instils loyalty.

Trying to apply Portunist principles to such a difficult enterprise would, you might think, show the flaws in the idea. In fact, it illustrates how viable the economic alternative is – perhaps showing that many economic alternatives would be. The realisation that changing the economic system is not only desirable, but is actually perfectly realisable, should be liberating in itself. Firstly, we are dealing with the apparent problem of scale for an enterprise like Man United. If Portunist restrictions in a 'small is beautiful' philosophy are applied to such an enterprise, how could it survive? Would it still be able to pursue its goals? (the next section comes with a pun warning)

Portunist policies (and we shall see the specific policies in the next section) would enforce a penalty for having excessively paid staff in the same enterprise with lowly or ordinarily paid staff. We will take the examples of a top striker and a groundsman.

Wayne Rooney is a British footballer famous for having a pair of feet that make him like a magician, and a pair of ears that make him like Shrek, with a talent for dramatic turnarounds so great that he can even make the hair on his head grow back. He was paid around £300,000 per week by his club in 2013. This is about 300 times as much as Tony Sinclair, the expert groundsman at the club, famous in the trade for his dedication and for having green-fingers as magical as Wayne's feet.

The details depend on the specifics of the policy, but with such high wage ratios there would be a hefty tax penalty to pay under the Limit policy if the enterprise did not react. And that penalty would inevitably harm the clubs ability to compete with other top clubs not under the same regime. So what to do?

Firstly, we can rule out the option of simply reducing the pay of the top players. Football may not be all about the money for many players, but with marked reductions in their pay, the talent would soon stop coming and so would the goals. Of course, if over time, Portunism caught on around the leagues of Europe and the world, moderation of the excessive salaries would not only be possible but would be inevitable. But we must find a solution for the short term, as that is where the critical economic risks reside for a radical new policy.

Manchester United employs under 1000 staff. Therefore, we can probably also rule out paying everyone £15m a year. So in the short term, the other logical option is to split the enterprise according to the cohorts of pay. For example, if the players, manager and coaching staff were in their own 'football talent' enterprise their business would not have wage ratios nearly so high. Likewise, a groundsman business might be a spin off, along with the back office, commercial operations and stadium workers, say. How this would work can be clarified by seeing what the best commercial options would be for the owners of United.

First of all some ground rules: You cannot simply put all the new business entities into the same group of companies. Policies would have to prevent this, otherwise that trick would quickly become the accounting strategy to avoid the restrictions. These must be genuinely separate businesses, each with autonomous objectives of their own. This is a big change in the way we are accustomed to think. So let us consider the consequences.

How can those completely separate enterprises work together and still succeed? For a genuine critique of our proposed system we need to understand just what sort of companies would be hiring Tony with his heavy roller and green fingers or Wayne with his heavy brow and green head. And what market forces would apply to those companies.

Market forces unleashed

Under Portunism alternative structures such as consumer ownership and cooperatives are important and should be nurtured. Mutualisation policies would be essential and cooperation through federations and collaboration would be commonplace. But breaking down the old behemoths into more agile networks must still allow people to come together with a big vision. A combined effort behind a united quest must still be capable of emerging from the networked pieces. And the break-up of morbidly obese enterprises, as one of the aims of Portunism, must not mean that the ambition or scale of human enterprise is limited.

And it need be no different for Manchester Federated Football Club. In the new businesses, Wayne and Tony both still want to focus on their jobs on the pitch and still want the same success for the club. In fact, the evidence is that, for large enterprises (larger than the famous football club) having a common goal for separate but related enterprises will result in greater success. In Part 3 Littlebelle gave the future-world example of the federation producing a national newspaper. Similar organisations have been proven with large consortia of scientific enterprises today. These are effective and innovative networks of firms and people where great human ambition for technical discovery and development are united and realised. Big firms, such as oil and pharmaceutical companies, that establish and run such consortia, already know that they could never be agile or creative enough to achieve this on their own.

Littlebelle also used the illustration of the enterprise with 'sight problems' to explain Professor Geoffrey West's conclusions that networks of smaller enterprises are more adaptable and are more efficient than the single corporation - constantly struggling with its inflexible internal network of interests. For a business losing its sight, eye surgery is dangerous, painful and often only partially successful. Whereas changing 'vision service provider' is fast, inexpensive and presents new opportunities.

So much for the structure of our new football club. What damage would this major reorganisation have on the market forces operating within such a network of spun off businesses?

Wayne is perhaps the easy case (as well as an easy target for cheap jibes by smug economics writers). As a sporting superstar he will always be rewarded grandly and his response is predictable too. Footballers are clearly endowed with canine levels of loyalty. They love their club, will applaud the faithful fans and devotedly 'play for the shirt', even kissing it when they score. That is until they get a better offer or they get caught in bed with the goal keeper's wife, of course. Just like the instincts behind such human waywardness, the market forces that reward those elite would change little at first.

But Tony and the business of pitch care are a different matter. Mr Sinclair would be encouraged to go freelance and setup a groundskeeping business – simply because that would save Wayne's firm a lot of money. With his specialist skills he would be invaluable to the club. You could argue that Wayne is paid millions because he makes the difference between winning and losing, but the same is almost true of Tony. Wayne and his manager have both commended the winning playing surface as well as blamed the pitch for losing matches in the past. So let us see how the market forces will play out on Tony's services?

The day they give Tony a pat on the back and a golden trowel as he leaves to setup Sinclair Groundskeeping Limited he will go home and think about the new contract he is about to sign. At this stage the club have few other options, so I think around £10m per year might be a reasonable fee to look after the famous turf. After all, world class pitches are needed for a world class performance on the pitch, and Man U. already spends millions leasing groundskeeping equipment. But this would still be a big shock to Mrs Sinclair as even top groundskeepers usually earn no more than £50k per year. This is how the market forces work today and this large disparity can be explained.

While employed, Tony was chosen from the best groundspeople, but from a traditional manual labour force that is not highly valued. In the agglomeration that was Man United the club has a 300:1 bias against the publicly invisible thick-armed Mr Sinclair, in favour of the likes of the publicly unmissable, thick-headed Mr Rooney. But when Tony first goes self-employed, the market forces operate without reference to prejudices against those working with their hands and without the historical backdrop of an industrial revolution ousting the balanced agrarian economy in favour of a northern English industrial sprawl. I admit this historical angle might be reading a bit too much into it, but still, it is a big change when Tony goes independent. And at first, he rakes it in.

But the amount Tony can charge will change. When

other companies, say from the tennis court or golf course industries, enter the market, encouraged by the new freer, competitive environment, an entire new branch of Professional Sport Groundskeeping is launched and Sinclair's Ltd will have to compete as hard as Man United do to stay at the top. The net result of these market forces is that Wayne can still play on a pitch as smooth as his pre-transplant head and Tony remains well respected and paid accordingly. But importantly, other lesser clubs can also benefit from excellent pitch care services from the new industry. And meanwhile the ridiculous amounts of money in football have been spread more evenly to other workers in, quite literally, wider fields.

Changing motivations

But what of the other companies spun out from and federated with the club? Perhaps there would be a loss of loyalty if a break-up meant they could also work for other football clubs?

Tony Sinclair is a lifelong fan of the team and so, I imagine, are many of the staff at Manchester United. When the jobs come up I suspect the most fervent fans are at the front of the hiring line. As the less football focussed work drifts off into other industries, just like Sinclairs' Limited did, that fanatical devotion could be lost. Does it matter? Would secretarial staff deliberately misspell a memo or trained accountants forget to claim the tax back on lawn feed, just because it was for their Man City client and not their beloved United? I doubt it. In any case, if there is a real conflict of interest, that staff member could be assigned to their favourite client, or clubs could chose an alternative firm or require an anti-conflict policy for their service companies. Conflicts of interest can be avoided.

The fact is that some jobs, like salesman, barrister (or centre-forward) require a degree of passionate loyalty to their customers (or fans) but most just require that near-universal desire to do a good job for a decent wage. Therefore any cohort of wage level in an enterprise could be separated if the owners chose to and there appear to be no fundamental obstacles to having these once integral functions spun out, scaled down and competing freely.

But would owners really take the convenient decision to split up their huge enterprise or would they find a way to avoid it?

Almost certainly owners and managers of today favour running the whole large enterprise - especially if it adds a degree of protection and potency to their dealings. This brings us onto the 'bucking the market' question – Are the market forces just too damn irresistible? For this question there are two things at issue. Perhaps managers, being part of the unbuckable, would be able to avoid the changes? Or perhaps Portunism, being unable to buck the market, would be forced to slash the wrist of the invisible hand, as Marxist economies have done in the past, and thereby kill off the benefits of free-competition and evolution.

To the first question, the main answer is that Portunism's aims are in no way trying to 'buck the market'. The advantages of a portunist-induced break-up are clear and the changes in what the enterprise is meant to do – from scoring goals to making electric toasters – will be minimal. The backroom staff will still be counting the money and paying the bills. The ground staff will still be watering and rolling the turf. And the footballers will still be rolling in the penalty area in balletic interpretations of a dying swan. In any case, Portunism is trying to open up competition and new markets - not buck them. The traditional 'can't buck the market' argument of neoliberalism and unfettered capitalism is an argument against central planning. Portunism has no central planning.

It was central planning that was roundly rebutted and quite successfully warded off by the likes of Freidrich

Hayek in the "Socialist calculation debates" of the 20th Century.[12] But what Portunism demands is a rebalancing of the control some individuals have, not central control and certainly not Hayek's Nemesis, Market Socialism. The rebalancing is needed to apply a counter pressure on the diseased free market system; not replace it.

And finally, what if managers presented with the challenge of responding to a new economic ideology, do not see it that way? What if they feel threatened, as is quite likely, as the powerful office that they once held is pushed to the brink? If those defiant managers represent the market that cannot be bucked, Portunism could have a problem. In the Manchester United example one can imagine that top clubs, instead of splitting up and federating their concerns, might try to find a way around the change. Let us look at the club owner's defensive options.

(1) They could pay players the same as before but illegally; (2) they could find creative new incentives beyond the reach of the tax man, instead of those excessive salary rewards that will be penalised; and (3) they could do a mixture of (1) and (2). If we judge that option (2) will inevitably partially succeed, meaning that other incentives are likely to be found, contributing to the inextricable will of the invisible hand, the simple conclusion would be that the Portunist policies are not a straightjacket.

What of it? The policies can still apply the necessary pressure to make enterprises smaller. The larger and more unequal the enterprise the greater would be the pressure, regardless of how much the once-elite are given little advantages. It would even probably improve our culture if rewards ceased to be exclusively the cash kind. This still puts an end to unrestricted and damaging growth and it still allows enterprises to compete as normal – even Manchester Federated.

A partial appraisal

The advantages of smaller business far outweigh the disadvantages. In particular, the major long term advantage in the football example, as in the wider business context, is the increasing competition and opportunity that would moderate excessive rewards. Football-lovers and egalitarians alike would probably agree this would not be a bad thing. As with top CEOs and bankers, the level of pay they receive has deeply offended much of society. Top footballers in the 1960's used to be paid around £1,300 per week (in today's prices) not £300,000 per week and the games were just as entertaining without the £100 haircuts and diva behaviour.

And the advantages that are claimed here for scaling down big business and spinning out new smaller enterprises from the old, are not new or overly optimistic. This is standard divestment and demerging that has been widely employed by very large forward thinking enterprises in Europe since at least the 1980's, and is also successfully employed when privatising and opening up large public sector organisations to more competition. Here, a prominent sporting team has been picked out only as an example. Football, with its apparently pampered and hugely paid players, may seem like an easy target for economic indignation, but actually if it were put in the dock for the crime of perverted economic evolution it may not have a case to answer. Overpaid divas are a systemic problem only when those divas also control the enterprises. Footballers do not. But in most very large enterprises dangerous divas are in charge. And we can put a stop to it.

So far we have only looked at a few of the most likely and popular objections to Portunism's challenge to neoliberalism. But there are many more that could be levied against it. For example, what about the practicalities of a Limit policy for companies where there are large differences in age and experience? What about the need for people to change companies in order to gain a pay rise? How will those companies retain the better staff? There are also more positive side-affects to be questioned. What will people use to measure their status against each other if income, and by extension consumer spending, becomes much more equalised? And what of the advantages to workers of companies having to do more to retain staff?

This introduction and provocation is not the place to address each challenge or to second-guess every objection that may come up in debate. But in each case there is every reason to believe there are solutions to the problems. What is for sure is that neoliberalism is not the only way, and the power of evolution and the proven ability for imaginative, free and enterprising people mean we can be confident that solutions will be found.

In addition, for every objection there is at least one added advantage of our proposed policies. For example, the Limit policy applied evenly across all ages and levels of experience may seem to disadvantage the experienced and without a more sophisticated tax penalty it would certainly favour the young. But the corresponding advantage, in this case, quickly becomes apparent.

142

Consider the evolution of our current system and how hierarchies have come to dominate. Consider also that within those hierarchies it takes years to work oneself up the ladder if that ladder is designed to be high, and that it is the same old bosses that set the value the firm puts on experience and conformity over youth and innovation. Then it follows that some of the advantages and additional rewards that the older and more experienced have are self-serving. Meaning our new policies could also provide a revitalised culture of vigorous creative new thinking by de-biasing the influence of the old and providing greater incentives and opportunities for the young.

One further advantage for the debate (although there are many): With flatter, less hierarchical enterprises the status and quality of many jobs would improve. Instead of large companies being able to exist by centralising creativity and decision making at head office while hiring bored teenagers to do the work of monkeys in the branches, they would be forced to devolve creativity and opportunity out to where the real value is added. Running a restaurant, for example, used to involve: responsibilities for the menu; for customer care; for hiring; for buying ingredients; and for promoting the establishment – varied, challenging and rewarding work. Now, with the advent of globalisation and the super-enterprise, running a restaurant often means no more than getting a different coloured cap and a badge that says "Team Leader".

Portunism, with such beneficial changes as these and many more - such as redirecting avoided tax from global companies back into the grass roots; such as introducing smaller, more localised industry; such as wasting less in transportation; such as greater diversity and innovation - all give us the chance to turn the clock back to ways of business that have been eroded to nothing over the last

40 or so years by a progressive degenerative disease, killing our communities and destroying the soul of the individual.

The final section in this book lists those specific Portunist policies within the SLIM framework that can be applied to deliver a future with transparency, equality and thriving networks of diverse enterprises.

For manifestos

At this crossroads for capitalism, the policies that our governments adopt for the management of business and our economies in the next ten years are likely to shape our culture, the natural environment and our freedoms and prosperity, for the next hundred. The following policies are determined steps towards a Portunist approach which are realisable and practicable today. They are divided into the four main objectives of the framework:

Separate

Limit

Internalise

Mutualise

Separate

To start the divergence of the unnaturally mated and convoluted economies of people and of business:

Create and establish a new currency for the human economy to operate in parallel to the business economy by progressively trialling methods such as:

- *Initially providing tax incentives for operating in the "folks currency"*

- *Piloting dual currencies in cities and regions*
- *Supporting the targeted adoption of cryptocurrencies*

Make B2B business and cash incompatible and remove old business coinage from the system

Establish the regulatory and legislative framework to illegalise the use of business money for personal use within a few years of the start of the folks currency alternatives

Limit

To enforce intra-enterprise equality in order to counter the expansive and exploitative forces deriving from human nature:

Modify personal tax laws to apply progressive evolutionary forces within the enterprise, investigating options such as:

- *Penalty-only limit forces applied only to over average earners in the enterprise*
- *Penalty-and-reward limiting forces for over average and under average earners*
- *Sliding scale penalties based on the size of enterprise or other metrics*
- *Fixing penalty and reward rates on different industries*
- *And special policies for the public sector, cooperatives and mutuals*

Bolster the application of tax laws around personal services masquerading as a company

Establish industry classifications for businesses for alternative limiting mechanisms (in the same way that fishermen and construction workers, for example, commonly are now)

Intern

To elevate the status of the peoples' economy and protect it from contamination by the business economy:

Ensure businesses register as B2B, B2C enterprises and individuals and sole traders treated as C2B or C2C enterprises

Establish controlled processes for the exchange to folks' money for the payment of staff

Setup and regulate currency exchanges for the trade of folks' and firms' money

Enforce a ban on unrestricted foreign exchange of folks' money

Monitor all purchases of folks' money and detect and prosecute abuse

Introduce and enforce rules to ensure the even distribution of profit across a group of companies, or add significant tax disincentives for not doing so

Mutualise

To allow new businesses to grow and prosper without violating the Limit Principle:

Establish through trials, viable mechanisms for setting investor-worker discount rates, including compulsory upper bounds; or rate setting by free competition for labour; and especially combining both

Establish transparent worker-owner cooperatives in the public sector that are competitive as suppliers and can successfully compete with the private sector for staff

Over time, expand mutualisation in the public sector so to keep pace with equality advances in the private sector

As limits on wage ratios constrict and expand to businesses that are adding investment, legislate for workers to have the right to choose between mutualisation and wage ratio limits

In time, assimilate into general employment law, the right to ramping mutual ownership in lieu of Limit rights

Apply special mutualisation rules to publicly floated businesses

"We cannot solve our problems with the same thinking we used when we created them."

– Albert Einstein

For comment and discussion:
www.utternomics.com

References

[1] **The Theory of Moral Sentiments**. Adam Smith. (1759)

[2] **Adapt. Why Success Always Starts with Failure.** Tim Harford. *Hachette Digital* (2011)

[3] **The Toaster Project, Or A Heroic Attempt to Build a Simple Electric Appliance from Scratch.** Thomas Thwaites. *Princeton Architectural Press* (2011)

[4] **An Enquiry into the Nature and Causes of the Wealth of Nations − Book I** *(Ch.10: Of Wages and Profit in the Different Employments of Labour and Stock.* Adam Smith. (1776)

[5] **Genetic Programming, On the Programming of Computers by Means of Natural Selection.** John R. Koza. *MIT Press* (1992)

[6] **The STEM Crisis Is a Myth**. Robert Charette. *IEEE Spectrum* (August 2013)

[7] **Emergence, From Chaos to Order**. John Holland. *Addison-Wesley* (1997)

[8] **Unravelling the mechanisms of trapline foraging in bees.** Lihoreau, Raine, Reynolds, Stelzer, Lim, Smith, Osborne and Chittka. *Communicative & Integrative Biology 6:1, e22701*; (January/February 2013)

[9] **The Use of Knowledge in Society. Individualism and Economic Order.** Friedrich Hayek. *The University of Chicago Press* (1948)

[10] **Urban scaling and its deviations: Revealing the structure of wealth, innovation and crime across cities.** Bettencourt, Lobo, Strumsky and West. *PLoS ONE* (2010)

[11] **A General Model for the Origin of Allometric Scaling Laws in Biology**. West, Brown, *Enquist. Science 276 [5309]* (1997)

[12] **Socialist Calculation III. The Competitive 'Solution'.** Friedrich Hayek. *Individualism and Economic Order. The University of Chicago Press* (1948)

www.ingramcontent.com/pod-product-compliance
Lightning Source LLC
Chambersburg PA
CBHW060035210326
41520CB00009B/1134